Total Frat
Move

Total Frat Move

W. R. Bolen

& THE CREATORS OF
TotalFratMove.com

GRAND CENTRAL
PUBLISHING

NEW YORK   BOSTON

Grand Central Publishing
Hachette Book Group
237 Park Avenue
New York, NY 10017

HachetteBookGroup.com

Printed in the United States of America

RRD-C

First Edition: January 2013

10 9 8 7 6 5 4 3 2 1

Grand Central Publishing is a division of Hachette Book Group, Inc.
The Grand Central Publishing name and logo is a trademark of Hachette Book Group, Inc.

The Hachette Speakers Bureau provides a wide range of authors for speaking events. To find out more, go to www.hachettespeakersbureau.com or call (866) 376-6591.

The publisher is not responsible for websites (or their content) that are not owned by the publisher.

Library of Congress Cataloging-in-Publication Data
Bolen, W. R.
    Total frat move / W. R. Bolen & the creators of TotalFratMove.com. — 1st ed.
        p. cm.
    Summary: "In the bestselling tradition of Tucker Max and Maddox comes TOTAL FRAT MOVE - the next (d)evolution in college debauchery, based on the highly popular website and twitter feed." — Provided by the publisher.
    ISBN 978-1-4555-1503-5 (hardcover) — ISBN 978-1-4555-1504-2 (trade pbk.) — ISBN 978-1-4555-1505-9 (ebook) — ISBN 978-1-61113-005-8 (audiobook)
    1. College students—United States—Conduct of life—Humor.   2. Greek letter societies—United States—Humor.   I. TotalFratMove.com.   II. Title.
    PN6231.C6B65 2013
    808.87'992–dc23
                                                            2012032116

Where fraternities are not allowed,
communism flourishes.

—Barry M. Goldwater, misquoted
by a reporter at the
Baltimore Catholic Review

Contents

From the Editors

This book has been fictionalized for the sake of narrative. We assure you, though, that variations of everything you're about to read are taking place in fraternities across America each and every semester. The photos that end each chapter are real. Identifying characteristics have been blurred to protect identities.

Total Frat Move

Join or Die a GDI

WHEN I WAS GROWING UP MY DAD ALWAYS TOLD ME, "Townes, college will be the best four years of your life." He was rarely wrong about anything, so I couldn't have been more excited to head off to school. High school was the minor leagues, and I was ready for the big show. Ready to walk onto the field under the lights, throw up on home plate, kick the catcher in the balls, and charge the mound. My parents made the trip with me to see that I was properly set up in my dorm, and to put a small buffer between unpacking and the start of a long binge-drinking career. They rode in my dad's Suburban, equipped with a trailer that contained everything I needed to recover from a hangover in comfort. I followed them in my truck as part of my dad's strategy to delay my mom's inevitable emotional breakdown.

I was rooming in Manor Hall, the most sought-after dorm for incoming freshmen due to its prime location and reputation for employing lenient resident advisors. It housed over a thousand first-year students, which made moving in complete chaos. Luckily, the female scenery was enough to make it bearable. If the prospect of being freed from parental shackles wasn't enough to get me pumped about college, the hundreds of eighteen-year-old slampieces who were now my neighbors definitely did the trick. They scampered back and forth with boxes from their parents' SUVs to their rooms, eager to start their lives as independent young women. Their fathers trudged back and forth despairingly, carrying suitcases filled with clothes that would eventually end up on the floor of some sexually inventive male classmate's bedroom.

While my dad and I carried my dresser, flat-screen, minifridge, and boxed-up belongings from our trucks to my room, my mom, Debbie Prescott, lounged in the dorm lobby reading brochures about student organizations and the health center. After an hour of unpacking it was finally time for goodbyes. I walked my mom to the car with my arm around her while she rambled about getting involved in student government and shoved pamphlets into the pockets of my shorts.

"I know you'll do great things here, honey. Your father and I love you very much and know you'll make good decisions. I miss you already."

"I'll miss you too, Mom, and I'll be fine," I said. "You have nothing to worry about."

Before leaving me to confront my destiny, my dad shook my hand, looked me square in the eye, and left me with some words of wisdom.

"Be good, kiddo. Don't do anything I wouldn't do."

"Yes sir," I said as our prolonged handshake struck an agreement between father and son.

Before getting into the car my mom swelled with sentiment, and as she fought back tears she whispered some emotional lyrics she stole from a bad country song.

"I hope you dance, Townesy."

She held me at arm's length and made high-pitched crying noises as her eyes watered, then turned without a word and slumped dramatically down into her seat. Before departing, my dad honked the horn and said, "Check your golf bag. I left you something in the side pocket." Then he peeled off into the sunset. Once they were out of sight I walked back inside and took the elevator to my room, sat on the polyester prefurnished couch surrounded by boxes, and took a deep breath. I knew I had just crossed the threshold into a new world. It was as if God had opened up the heavens, shot me a thumbs-up with a wink, and said, *Go forth, my son, and spread your seed, for I have instilled a spirit of triumphant rage within you.* I reached into our still unplugged mini-fridge, grabbed two warm Keystones, and tossed one to my roommate, Monte.

Monte was a six-foot-five man-child, whose Christian name was Peter Montgomery. He was an all-state middle linebacker our senior year of high school, but had always been too smart for his size, so he turned his back on the pigskin to focus on his education after getting a full ride to college. We had been best friends since sixth grade, when our dads started a law firm with a few other lawyer buddies. Monte's longtime high school girlfriend, Sarah, had gotten into some out-of-state school, and like all young couples who think they can make it work, they were determined to maintain a healthy long-distance relationship. Fucking stupid.

The beer I tossed his direction thudded against Monte's chest and rolled into his lap. He looked at me, disgruntled, and I offered a resolution.

"Let's get shitfaced."

"Shouldn't we unpack first?" he asked.

I pretended not to hear his question and chugged my beer before spiking it to the floor, unknowingly starting a trend that would lead to us having the filthiest dorm room in the history of civilized domiciles. Monte followed suit.

"All right, that was a good start, but I'm unpacking and calling Sarah before we do anything else." He wiped his mouth and took out his phone.

While he unpacked and called Sarah, probably to vow undying abstinence in her absence, I checked my bag to see what surprise my dad had left me. I reached into the side pocket, rustled through the customized Pro V1s with my TP3 logo, and pulled out an envelope. Inside was an American Express card and a note.

Townes,

College is a time for great personal growth. These are significant years you'll hold dear for the rest of your life. You're a Prescott. Carry our family name with the same respect as the generations before you. The Alpha house is a great place, and you're going to make a lot of mistakes there that your mother can never hear about. I made friendships and connections during my stay that helped shape me into the man I am today. Remember, above all else, you're there to learn.

TPII

P.S. Take the hazing like a man.

If he had any idea what would transpire over the next several hours, or how crazy I'd go with that AmEx over the next several years, that letter would've been comprised purely of threats and curses.

As I folded the letter back into the envelope, I heard the

scamper of feet outside our door, followed by a series of unusually polite knocks.

"Who is that? The fucking RA already?" I asked Monte.

He was still talking to Sarah, so he put his hand over the phone and waved me off apathetically to check the door.

I walked over and looked through the peephole.

Darkness.

"Who is it?" I asked loudly.

I heard muffled giggling and a series of much louder knocks in response.

I glanced around our room to make sure we didn't have anything illegal visible, and cracked open the door to investigate. Four girls in all black shoved their way through, shrieking like cats in heat. Two of them bum-rushed me as I covered my ears and stumbled backward.

"Mother of God," Monte said as his jaw dropped and he quickly hung up on Sarah.

The first thing I noticed was how incredibly hot and blonde they were. They playfully pushed me to the ground, and in my confused state I chose to let them have their way with me. I put up enough of a fight to make it fun for them, but I wanted to see where this was going. One of them bound my hands with rope behind my back while the other stretched duct tape over my mouth. My mind raced to figure out what the hell was going on, and then one of the girls wiped the confusion from my face with a glorious explanation.

"You're being kidnapped, sweetie," the blonde assassin informed me like a slutty psychic mind reader.

"Can I tie you up next?" I mumbled through the tape.

Monte had scrambled into a fortified position atop his bed. He was wildly swinging his pillow at two attackers, determined to delay the inevitable. Once he noticed my lack of resistance he laid down his defense and conceded defeat.

"Don't worry," assured the girl with two trophy-worthy tits, "we'll take good care of you."

I probably looked like a kid in a candy store, eyes aglow with bewilderment and anticipation. Monte looked like a man who had forgotten the safe word during an S&M sex act gone horribly wrong.

"Welcome to college, boys," the ringleader announced as she eye-fucked my face off. "We're taking you to the Alpha house for the annual Paint Your Toga party."

I lit up like the first time a girl gripped my shaft, and nodded my wide-eyed approval. When I was a senior in high school I'd heard rumors about this hybrid toga/paint rush party, and it sounded like an orgy with multicolored lube. The girls pulled me to my feet and hit the lights as we left the room before Monte and I even had a chance to settle in.

Other kids on our floor gasped and laughed, carrying boxes filled with Bob Marley posters and Hot Pockets as we were rushed through the hallways toward the exit. Outside, a brand-new black Tahoe with a flower lei hanging from the rearview came to a screeching halt in front of us.

"Throw them in the back!"

Another hot blonde. They were multiplying.

The trunk door automatically opened, and we clumsily ducked our way in just in time before it slammed behind us and the driver sped off.

"Okay, guys! I'm Allison Kimball and I'm a Pi," said the girl with the immaculate set of twins as she reached over the backseat and applied a blindfold to my eyes.

"Totally sorry for the drama, but we always kidnap rushees

for the first party of the year. What are your names? Oh, silly me. Duct tape."

She ripped the tape from Monte's face first.

"Fuck," he said under his breath. "Peter Montgomery... Monte. Nice to meet you ladies."

I felt the tape tear peach fuzz from my upper lip.

"Townes Prescott," I said. "This is awesome."

"Oh, so *this* is the Townes we've heard so much about," said one of the girls in the front of the vehicle.

I'd only been there for six hours and already had a reputation, no doubt thanks to my dad's contributions to the Alpha fraternity house.

"Let's get this party started!" one of them squealed.

Suddenly an obnoxious Taylor Swift song was blaring through the speakers, and someone tugged my hair to tilt my head back.

"Open your mouth, sweetie," Allison said seductively in my ear.

I opened up like a baby bird awaiting its first meal, and whiskey flooded my taste buds and dripped down my chin. I momentarily pitied the guys in their dorm rooms trying to level up on World of Warcraft. They would always be GDIs (god damn independents), and never experience the pure thrill of being kidnapped by hot sorority girls. My empathy ended when I heard Monte sputter up some liquid, and I could tell he was also being waterboarded with whiskey. Moments later my hair was yanked again and this time I tasted tequila. This process was repeated several more times before we finally came to a stop. Another masculinity-threatening song raped my ears until I was finally pulled from the car, and I accidentally head-butted Monte in the face on the way out.

"SHIT, TOWNES!"

"Watch your language in front of the ladies, you fucking jackass," I snapped back.

I stumbled without sight from the SUV, trying to find my legs, when suddenly the blindfold was pulled from my eyes. Sunlight flooded my retinas as I squinted and tried to make out my surroundings. As the foreground focused, my eyes took in an incredible, well-manicured lawn. In the background, an enormous mansion began to take shape.

"Thank you, God," I said under my breath. "It's beautiful."

I had seen pictures of my dad at the house, but nothing could prepare me for the breathtaking moment in which I absorbed its magnificence firsthand. In the middle of Greek Row on a sprawling lot, from the outside it looked like a massive southern plantation home with towering columns. Driving by you would never think, *Hey, that's a place where hundreds of young people absorb unholy amounts of alcohol and try to invent new sex positions*, but that's exactly what it was. A glorious mansion where dreams came true and wild fantasies were fulfilled.

Less than an hour at college had passed. We were there. Rush had begun. This was it.

While I was born in the greatest country in the world (America, fuck yeah), and into a great family (Prescott, fuck yeah), I wasn't born into my fraternity. Trust me, if anyone could've been I would've been, but no man is born wearing his letters. However, being a legacy with a handshake like a fucking arm-wrestling champion certainly boosted my status as a sought-after shoo-in during rush. Fraternity recruitment can be surprisingly similar to that of a successful collegiate football program. In order to field a respectable pledge class you have to get everyone shitfaced and show them how much ass they'll get if they commit. Much of what goes on is completely against university rules and state laws, but if you're not cheating you're not trying. Monte and I had been contacted by Alpha's rush chairman several times throughout the summer to ensure our involvement. I had been looking forward to this since I saw Otter fuck the dean's wife in *Animal House* when I was seven years old. Nothing could keep me from it.

Now I was being ushered toward the back porch with Allison on my arm. After a few steps I realized I was already buzzing hard.

"We don't even have togas," Monte pointed out.

"Don't worry about that," Allison explained. "One of these guys will take care of y'all."

We were immediately greeted by several upperclassmen who looked like participants in a political debate who had gotten lost and ended up at a toga party. Their heads were adorned with ivy and they were all wearing penny loafers or boat shoes. The lankiest of the five was clad in an American flag bedsheet, and he handed me a fifth of Kentucky Deluxe before throwing a white sheet and some rope over my shoulder.

"You're Townes, right? Russell Atwater, rush chair. We talked on the phone last week. It's great to finally meet you in person."

He extended his hand for a shake, and I gave him a firm grip. Then we squared off in a manly staredown as an unspoken shootout of confidence took place, which resulted in mutual respect. We were telepathically acknowledging, *I'm not a fucking pussy and you understand that because neither are you.* The agreement ended with a slight nod.

"All right then," he said. "Change into your togas and throw your clothes into the back of my truck and let's go get fucking wasted."

We quickly changed as Atwater flirted with our female escorts.

"Holy shit, this is going to be fucking incredible," I said to Monte as I wrapped myself in the bedsheet.

He just nodded, still too rattled from the abduction to decide how he felt. We tossed our shirts into the back of the truck and walked back over to the group.

"I'll give you a tour of the house and we'll meet some of the other guys," Atwater said. "The band comes on in under an hour, so I hope you gentlemen are ready to get fucking rowdy."

"We're heading back to our place to change, but we'll see you later," said Allison, smiling back at me as she walked away with the other girls.

We headed up the sidewalk and up the back staircase onto a massive outdoor balcony where we were consumed by a sea of togas. Creedence Clearwater Revival was rocking through speakers positioned above the wooden deck. As we made our way through the crowd we passed several girls whose "togas" weren't really togas at all. Instead, with any fabric deemed unnecessary having been strategically cut away, they exposed as much skin as possible. I had yet to see a single one that I wouldn't punch Monte in the dick just to make out with. Apparently Mr. Committed Relationship was enjoying the scenery too, because I noticed him staring at a brunette who was a few centimeters of toga fabric away from a nip slip.

"Still miss your girlfriend, you dickhead?" I asked. "Save us both the trouble, call her now and tell her you need a break for at least the next twelve hours."

"It's our first night here, I think I can show a little restraint."
His eyes stayed focused on the brunette, who was clearly
enjoying our attention.

Atwater overheard us talking and stopped in his tracks.

"Wait, this big fucking idiot has a *girlfriend*?"

"Yeah, we've been together for over two years," Monte
explained like a loyal poodle. "She goes to Vandy."

"HAHA!" Atwater seemed pleased with the situation. "Do
you realize how much strange ass is going to get thrown at you
tonight? Give in to the temptation; you'll be a better man for
it. Look around you. It's like a buffet, for fuck's sake."

Monte let out a worrisome chuckle.

We made our way into the house, where the walls, ceiling,
and floors were covered in black tarp to protect against the
impending paint explosion. The distinct smell of grain alcohol
and a hundred years of historic sex filled my nostrils. Everywhere I looked there was someone with a can, bottle, or cup
upended. As we walked through the corridor I noticed a girl
with her legs wrapped around a guy wearing nothing but a kilt,
making out with a drunken passion like I'd never seen before.

"That's Scott McCandles," Atwater explained. "When he
blacks out he ditches whatever he was wearing and throws on
that kilt."

"That chick is licking his forehead, so it seems to be working for him," I said as we walked past.

We were approaching the staircase when suddenly a lunatic
in a cowboy hat and toga came flying down the stairs at 20
mph riding an ironing board like a sled. He hit the ground
and skidded into the wall, spilling his drink everywhere and
knocking his head. Behind him followed ten guys with black
trash bags full of mischief.

"That's the president," said Atwater. "Sean Harvey."

"What's in the bags?" I asked. The volume of the party forced us to raise our voices.

"Tubes of paint," said Atwater. "Those bags will be spread out on the dance floor, so once the band starts playing you just grab some and go apeshit."

"I never want to leave this place!" Monte proclaimed to no one in particular. A fascinated smile stretched across his face as the booze began to loosen him up.

We made our way up the stairs and down a long corridor with bedrooms to the left and right. Everything on the second floor was covered in tarp as well. The house was even bigger than I initially realized, and we turned a corner down another long hallway before finally reaching Atwater's room. There was a sign on his door written in sharpie that read RUSHEES AND TITS, OTHERWISE: GET THE FUCK OUT. He kicked the door open and there were already several guys inside drinking and talking.

"All right, y'all go around and meet the other rushees and take some shots or whatever," said Atwater as he headed toward his bathroom. "Help yourselves."

Monte and I ended up shooting whiskey with Nathan Johnson and Tim Rumsen, who were both rushing as well. They both had the same look of eager readiness on their faces. After briefly taking part in standard introductory protocol, Nathan cut to the chase.

"You can call me Nate," he said. "Tim here has some blow if you're into that."

I had ingested my fair share of illegal substances in high school, but I wasn't totally sold on hitting party powder at my first collegiate event. Just as I opened my mouth to tell them we appreciated the offer but no thanks, Monte chimed in.

"Why not?"

Then Atwater came out of nowhere and put his arm over my shoulder.

"Nose candy? I'm in."

It was the perfect snowstorm of peer pressure. My mind wandered for a split second as I wondered if my parents had safely completed their journey home, and then Atwater handed me a rolled-up $20 bill. I looked over at Monte, who was already wide-eyed and smiling like a white-nostriled Jim Carrey, nodding his approval.

Fuck it. If Monte's punk ass can handle it, so can I.

I leaned over, put President Andrew Jackson to my nose, and railed a line off Atwater's iPad.

Just as my brain went into overdrive, I heard the band kick off the night through the floorboards with "Born in the USA," and suddenly Tim sprinted out down the hall without saying a word.

"Well, Tim is fucking awesome," said Monte, rubbing his nose.

We looked to Atwater for our next move. His bloodshot eyes darted around the room while he searched for meaningful words to motivate us, and then he delivered an eloquent speech I'll remember for the rest of my life.

"If you get lucky and my room is unlocked you can fuck on the floor. Otherwise just try random doors."

He bent down, inhaled another line, put one fist high in the air, and marched out of his room like a general leading his troops into battle. I gulped down the last of my whiskey drink and followed him out to plunge headfirst into a lifestyle that I would maintain for over half a decade.

We made our way downstairs and over to one of the make-shift bars where beers were being handed out like United

Nations survival packs in an African war zone. I noticed Atwater grabbing cans and shoving them down into his toga.

"You're going to want extras!" he yelled over the music.

I followed his lead, tucking two into the pockets of my shorts under my toga and taking two in each hand. I turned to hand one to Monte, but he was gone. After stocking up, we pushed through the crowd, which had tripled in size since our arrival, and made our way toward the massive dining room where the band was located. I saw Tim out the corner of my eye scooping a cup full of reddish-pink liquid from a twenty-gallon trash can.

"Pink panty-dropper punch," Atwater explained. "It's really just for girls, but some real degenerates who like blacking out immediately are into it."

Tim was obviously the latter. I was already shit-hammered, so I had no need for girly pink disaster liquid. We maneuvered through one last wave of people and turned the corner into the giant party room. Girls were frolicking in circles and squeezing entire tubes of paint onto each other's heads. Guys were full-sprinting across the room and sliding headfirst like Pete Rose at high speeds across the paint-covered canvas that protected the wood flooring.

Suddenly a multicolored person raced past me, flailing both arms wildly in a figure eight across his body, and paint splattered across my face and chest.

"It's go time!" yelled Atwater as he wiped a glob of green from his cheek and took off in the direction of the stage.

"We need some fucking paint!" Nate shouted in my ear.

I nodded in agreement and we made our way through the madness toward the closest trash bags, our togas becoming less white with every step. Soon we would be part of a drunken rainbow race like the rest of the room. The look of joy that this decadent environment put on my face would've made my hometown pastor's head explode.

As I reached into the bag and grabbed from the assorted tubes of color, someone's hands covered my eyes. My drunken reflexes kicked in and I turned swiftly, ready to extinguish my attacker with a barrage of red and blue paint. My counterattack paused when I realized it was a girl. Her face was like every other in the crowd, purplish brown from the mix of primary colors, but Allison's ample mounds were easily distinguishable.

"It's me, stupid!" she screamed. "Let's go dance!" She took hold of my hand. "You need to get dirtier!"

Yes, we do.

She playfully ran her paint-covered hands through my hair and then pulled me toward the gathered masses. As we stumbled along I polished off one of my beers, handed another to her, and reloaded. We were in the middle of the dance floor when the band sent a flurry of piano keys through the air that caused everyone to crank up their intensity another notch into the code-red danger zone. It was Journey's "Don't Stop Believin'," and I was immediately swept up in the craziest dance party I'd ever been a part of.

Allison and I jumped up and down like little kids in an inflatable castle filled with booze. I chugged half of my beer and then swung the can wildly over my head, spraying everyone within a ten-foot radius and causing a chain reaction that resulted in around thirty other people beer showering simultaneously. I was performing a series of terrible white-guy dance moves (a combination of the twist and the classic water sprinkler) when I slipped on a slick puddle of paint, lost my footing, and landed on my back. I couldn't feel a thing, and alcohol refused to give awkwardness a chance to set in, so I embraced the moment and flailed around on the floor like I was having an epileptic seizure while Allison poured beer straight into my mouth like a fountain a few feet above me. It was pure glory. Nothing else in the world mattered. There were no parents, no rules, and no worries.

I stood back up when I'd had my fill, and the next thing I knew Allison and I were moving toward each other in drunken slow motion as I stiff-armed strangers blocking our embrace. What ensued on the dance floor could not be considered "slow dancing" by any legal definition, but was sloppily paced grinding that would've made her father regurgitate his dinner. An unopened beer fell from my waist to the tarp floor, and as I bent over to retrieve it I realized Allison had gone to grab it too, and I was inches from her face. This was my second "fuck it" moment of the night. The kiss that followed swapped a mixture of spit, beer, and paint. When our lips parted ways, the amount of alcohol in my system caused me to lose my footing and tumble to the ground again, pulling Allison down on top of me.

"You're crazy!" She laughed.

I ignored the accusation and decided on a game plan.

"You wanna go take some shots?" I asked, helping her to her feet.

"Absolutely! Where?"

"Atwater's room. He said I could help myself."

She took my hand and we headed out of the crowd toward the stairs. Right before we reached the steps I noticed another couple against the wall making out, except this time it wasn't Scott McCandles in his kilt.

The girl's toga was hiked up around her waist. The guy

had apparently lost his toga, wearing only khaki shorts that were now badly stained, and claw marks on his back that were apparently from her nails. While he shielded the dirty action of his hand below her waist from the wandering eyes of passersby, I noticed he was performing an act usually reserved for the privacy of a bedroom. Normally I would've laughed it off and kept to myself, but I came to a sudden, alarming realization. It was Monte.

"Holy shit, Monte, is that you?" I interrupted.

He looked back over his shoulder with a blank stare. There was no shame in his eyes as he attempted to form a smile with the alcohol-sedated muscles in his face. Any speck of remorse that he normally would've shown was hidden behind a curtain of booze and drugs.

"Are you fucking serious right now? In the hallway?"

I laughed hysterically as he finally realized who I was.

"Townes!" He faltered backward toward me. "What the fuck is up?" His slurred words were barely understandable.

"Monte?" His female companion was confused. "You said your name was Peter!"

He turned back to her to attempt an explanation as Allison tugged on my hand to lead me upstairs.

"Take it to a room, you fucking wildebeest," I yelled as I walked away.

Each step of the stairs was like a hurdle, and when we reached the top I decided there was no time to waste and took aim for the kill shot. We made out intermittently as we headed down the hallway and I said a mental prayer that Atwater's door would be unlocked. When we reached his room it was wide open, and someone was passed out facedown in his bed. Allison stopped outside and I walked in on a reconnaissance mission. His face was completely purple, but I knew it was Tim. Atwater's bed was covered in smears of paint, and his pillow was dribbled with Tim's punch-stained drool. He was still breathing, and I decided there was no reason to wake him. After all, Atwater had said to fuck on the floor.

"He's out cold," I informed Allison as I grabbed the closest bottle from the dresser. "Vodka?" I asked as she shut the door.

I poured a glass, but as I turned to hand it to her she pounced on me like a rabbit in heat. She pushed me up against the dresser and we tore at each other's togas, desperately searching for mutual nudity. When we were totally disrobed she slid to her knees and started fellating the only inches of my body not tainted with paint. Tim let loose a drunken groan in his sleep. I reached behind me and grabbed the glass to take one last swig of vodka before going in for some floor fucking. I didn't even have time to consider the fact that Atwater probably kept condoms in his dresser; things were moving too quickly.

I was only a few thrusts in when a loud *Kaboom* shook the ground like an earthquake, causing Allison to scream and Tim to shoot up suddenly like a zombie arisen from the dead.

"What the fuck was that?" Allison shrieked as she grabbed for her toga to cover herself.

"Shots fired?!?" Tim asked, only half conscious.

Just then Atwater kicked open his door.

"Some fucking idiot loaded the cannon with paint tubes and fired it!" he yelled.

He quickly realized I was popping my college cherry in his room.

"Townes? Nice!" He turned and looked at his bed. "Tim? What the fuck?"

I quickly helped Allison to the bathroom so she could get

dressed and slammed the door behind her as I pulled up my shorts and tried to find my bearings.

"There's a cannon? What the hell is happening?" I asked Atwater.

He briefly explained that the chapter had an old Civil War relic in the backyard, and someone thought it would be a good idea to pack it with gunpowder and tubes of paint before throwing a flaming piece of toilet paper inside. I was trying to digest the absurdity of the situation when Monte stumbled into the room behind him. He stood in the doorway, maintaining his stance with one arm on the wall, wearing his boxers, a few layers of paint, and a glob of drool hanging from his chin. Atwater took one look at him and decided we were a liability.

"You guys better get the fuck out of here, the cops will show up any minute. Take the fire escape." He grabbed Monte by the arm and ushered him toward the window.

I looked at the bathroom door, considering Allison's fate, but Monte had already begun his descent and there was no way I was letting that slapdick wander home alone. Atwater noticed my concern.

"Dude, I'll take care of her, get the fuck out of here!"

I was in no position to argue, so I headed for the window and looked out. Monte was about halfway down the ten-step ladder, and motioned for me to follow him. I climbed down and as my feet touched the ground I saw the flashing of red and blue lights coming from the front of the house. I crouched with my toga over my shoulder while Monte swayed in his boxers. Tim made it halfway down the ladder before losing his grip and flailing through the air like a wounded duck. He landed square on his back with his legs pointed straight up, bouncing his head off the grass.

"We're going to have to take a back route," whispered Monte. He was down on one knee, scanning the area and licking his lips furiously while he flashed his hands in different directions like a covert Navy SEAL. Tim got to his feet, unfazed by the fall, and gave Monte a thumbs-up in response.

A flashlight beamed around the side of the house, so we scrambled into the bushes.

"We'll jump the fence in the backyard and head for the alley behind Manor," I strategized.

"You think they're gonna shoot that cannon at us?" Tim asked.

Monte tapped my shoulder and we eased our way out of the bushes, but after a few feet I turned back to see Tim rooted to the ground with a look of pure horror on his face. A group of people covered from head to toe in red paint had turned the corner, followed by flashlights.

"Jesus Christ, it's a fucking massacre!" Tim cried out. "RUN! EVERYONE RUN!"

A flashlight beam hit Tim in the chest.

"Tim! Let's go! Now!" I yelled.

The flashlight hit me and I looked over at the cop standing directly below Atwater's room.

"Stop! Do not attempt to run!" he commanded.

The thought of calling my dad from jail less than twenty-four hours after leaving for school set off an alarm in my head. I ran back to Tim and jerked him by the arm. He tripped through the bushes and toppled into me, sending us both to the ground in a paint-stained heap. We were just feet away from the cop, tangled up and totally exposed. It was all over. But then fate took a turn.

The officer's eyes hardened as he reached for his handcuffs, but out of nowhere a colorfully coated and unidentifiable Alpha walked up and tapped him on the shoulder.

"This is private property," he said boldly. "Where's your probable cause?"

The cop spun around, taken off guard by what sounded like a lawyer and looked like a member of an art cult. The Alpha's legal rant continued as the officer's hand moved swiftly to his Taser holster.

"Where's your warrant?" he asked with a cocky head tilt.

"Step back and calm down," the cop said firmly.

The Alpha ignored him. "This is unconstitutional. I'm taking down your badge number."

He reached for the badge pinned to the cop's chest as the *Pop* of the Taser being fired echoed into the night sky.

"Arggghhhhhhh!" He went stiff and toppled toward the ground as the voltage coursed through his veins and spittle flew from his lips.

The cop dropped his knee into the guy's back as I pulled Tim to his feet and turned to sprint. Monte was already running like a bronze medalist in the Special Olympics for giants. Tim and I took off after him. We jumped a few fences and eventually found our way into an alley that led directly to our dorm. When we were a safe distance from the house I stopped to catch my breath.

"Holy shit!" I said, gasping. "Whoever that was, he saved our asses!"

"Sarah is going to disown me." The cannon fire, police, and adrenaline had brought Monte to the sobering reality that it had taken him less than twenty-four hours to fuck up.

"Man...you really did get carried away." I attempted to ease his mental anguish with a pat on the back. "She's never going to know."

We finally reached our building as a girl was swiping her ID to get inside. She looked at us like we were completely insane.

"You guys have a good night?" she asked, smirking.

"You have no idea," I responded.

When we were finally inside our room I immediately lay down on my bare mattress. My sheets and bedding were still in boxes. Monte face-planted onto his own bed, and Tim curled up on the floor using a trash bag filled with Monte's clothes as a pillow, still in shock from the gruesome scene he thought he'd witnessed.

"Welcome to college, Monte," I said.

"Fuck you, Townes," he said back.

Adrenaline still had me wired, so I stared up at the ceiling and waited for it to fade, listening to Tim violently snore in his sleep. Serenity washed over me knowing everything in my life was going perfectly according to plan. I'd gotten into school, moved into my dorm with my best friend, and been recruited on the first night by the fraternity I knew I wanted to join. Not to mention I'd managed to lose my collegiate virginity, even if just for a few pumps. I was ready to spend the rest of my time on campus racking up as many nights like this as I possibly could.

———

The beginning of college means one thing: the beginning of rush. A new group of freshmen floods in and unparalleled excitement sweeps over campus as the independent lives of the future leaders of America begin with the crack of thousands of beers. These TFMs embody this time period...

On Fraternity Rush and the Beginning of College

Back to school shopping at the liquor store. TFM.

Meeting people for the first time, multiple times. TFM.

The leaders of tomorrow being unable to remember last night. TFM.

Themed parties: the gentlemanly way of telling girls to wear something slutty. TFM.

Holding back your laughter when the recruitment chair tells the rushees "We have a strict zero tolerance policy when it comes to hazing." TFM.

Freshmen move-in, it's like Christmas, but for your penis. TFM.

GDI approached the door and tried to explain that his girlfriend was inside. I said, "There are a lot of guys' girlfriends inside," and slammed it shut. TFM.

What I called "that night of drinking where I almost died" in high school is now just called Thursday. TFM.

Enjoy the front seat of my car now rushee, you'll be in the trunk soon. TFM.

Twenty-one to drink, eighteenish to sleep over. TFM.

The beer pong dunk. TFM.

Blacking out and getting onstage with the band. TFM.

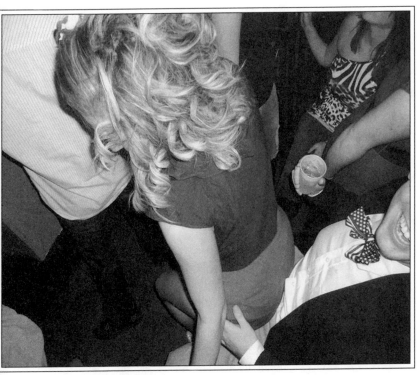

Dancing like you're not a well-off private school kid. TFM.

Passing out in the midst of the destruction. TFM.

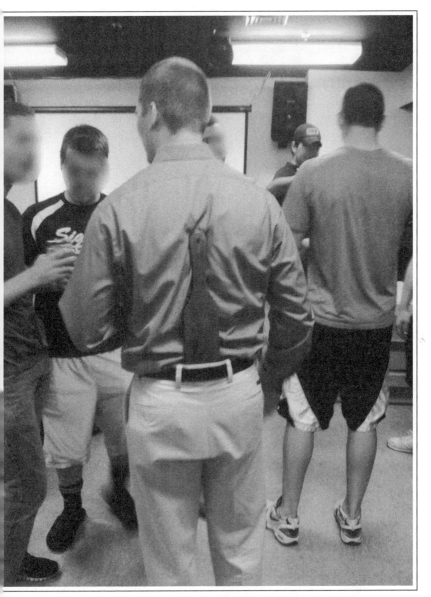

The rushees don't know what's coming, but it's coming. TFM.

The Ice Cream Social

RUSH CONTINUED FOR TWO WEEKS AFTER THAT LIFE-changing toga party kick-started my college career. Every night the Alphas gave us another reason to rage that tested both the limits of my liver and the elasticity of my jeans due to repetitive dance floor boner exposure. Thursday through Saturday the dorms emptied and the streets were littered with people headed to different parties. Girls were waved past the hired security at the entrance of the Alpha house, and the unfortunate guys who weren't on the rush list walked away staring at the ground.

Even on the rare weeknight that a party didn't break out at the house, Atwater and his recruitment captains took the rushees to dinner with a different group of sorority girls. And we didn't go out for chicken fingers and onion rings. It was always the back room at an upscale steakhouse where we could get obnoxious, or a sushi place where we would bang out sake bombs and slam Japanese beer. Everything was charged to the chapter credit card as part of the rush budget, and Atwater never even looked at the check before slapping down the plastic.

Their goal was to impress us, and it worked. School never even had a chance to become a priority. How could I give a shit about my history lecture knowing a few hours later I'd be double-fisting beers and singing "Tiny Dancer" at the top of my lungs with a girl under each arm? It was nonstop boozing, laughing, flirting, and fucking with zero consequences that felt like it would never end. Then, one fateful Friday, my phone rang and Atwater's name appeared on the screen.

I pulled my iPhone from my pocket and muted *SportsCenter* to answer his call.

"Townes, put on a blazer and slacks, pick up a gallon of your favorite ice cream, and head up to the house." His tone was far more serious than usual.

"Ice cream? What flavor do I—"

"Just pick a fucking flavor and be there by six o'clock sharp." *Click.*

None of the Alphas had ever expressed any emotion other than enthusiasm to get me sloppy drunk and laid, and I'd never heard Atwater sound even mildly irritated. I had no idea why he was acting like a dickhead.

I sat in silence, considering the possibilities, until Monte walked in from class and told me he just got the exact same call from one of the recruitment captains who assisted Atwater. "Rush might be over," he said as he slid one arm into his blazer.

"And we might be fucked," I replied. It was already 5:45, so I grabbed my coat and we headed into the parking garage to get my truck.

"Did he seem pissed off to you?" Monte asked.

"He hung up on me."

Neither of us said a word the rest of the way to the grocery store. My brakes squeaked as I swerved into a parking spot and we hustled inside to grab ice cream.

A few minutes later we arrived at the frat house with time to spare. The parking lot was overflowing with SUVs and trucks. Most had Alpha stickers on the rear window along with Ducks Unlimited or Coastal Conservation Association decals. We parked on the street as several other rushees were getting out of their cars, and I saw dozens of others in sport coats already standing around picnic tables set up on the front lawn.

We approached the tables and I realized that not a single active member of the fraternity was in the yard, just rushees. That's when I looked up and saw at least forty of the 110-man chapter packed onto the second-floor balcony, looming over us. They had beers in their hands and scowls on their faces, staring down like vultures at soon-to-be-dead prey.

I set my ice cream down on a table with countless other buckets, every one of them vanilla, and walked over to Tim to see if he knew what the Alphas had planned.

"Tell me you know what the fuck is going on here."

"I have no fucking idea," he said. "I was one of the first people to show, and when I tried to head upstairs one of the seniors was like, 'Stay in the fucking yard!' I feel like a dog in a $300 blazer."

I walked through the crowd, stopping and talking with guys I hadn't seen in a few days. One of the other rushees, Garrett Rogers, was in the middle of telling me how an RA walked in on him pounding a girl in her dorm's laundry room when a loud whistle from the upstairs balcony interrupted him. The president of Alpha, Sean Harvey, leaned over the railing with his hair neatly combed, wearing a navy blazer and a red tie with blue stripes. He put his fingers to his mouth and whistled once more, louder this time.

"Fellas, pay the fuck attention!" he yelled.

Everyone stopped talking and stared up at him.

"Today is a very important day in your lives," he began. "It is one that will change you forever if you accept the honor we bestow upon you. You'll notice that not all of the fucking free-loaders that have been coming to our parties are here today. That's because we've spent the last few weeks evaluating all of you, and those guys aren't Alpha material. *You*, however, are being invited to be a part of our fraternity. Congratulations to the forty-two of you on receiving bids from Alpha!"

In a split second all my worries turned to sheer, face-melting happiness. A chorus of congratulatory applause and roaring cheers rained down on us from the balcony, along with empty beer cans, packs of cigarettes, and a couple of lawn chairs. We rotated through one another, slapping backs and shaking hands with accomplishment in our swagger and acceptance in our smiles. Nate and Tim hugged it out. The ovation continued as I took a deep breath and let out a sigh of relief. I had been looking forward to this moment from the second I received my acceptance letter to the university. There was never any doubt I'd get in, but it was still a huge weight off my back knowing I was no longer a GDI.

President Harvey told us to take the next half hour to get to know each other in a sober environment for a change, and then Atwater stepped up to the railing and congratulated us.

"Enjoy that fucking ice cream, and if you're here in thirty minutes we'll assume you've accepted your bid. Congratulations on being invited into the best goddamn fraternity on this campus."

Robert Earl Keen was turned up full blast inside the house as Monte walked up and hit me in the arm so hard that my hand went numb. "I knew we weren't fucked, you jackass!"

We sat down at the table next to Nate and I grabbed a plastic spoon to dig into a melting tub of vanilla. I looked up at the balcony where the flock of actives had been staring down at us, but they were gone. My smile widened as I imagined them inside, setting up for the party of the century to welcome us as brothers.

Nate nudged me, drooling ice cream down his chin and grinning like a happy twelve-year-old sitting at the cool kids' table for the first time. "Tonight is going to be fucking classic. I'm getting a chubby just thinking about it!" I nodded in agreement as I slurped down another spoonful.

But suddenly Robert Earl Keen shut off mid-song and was replaced by harsh, screeching death metal appropriate for the intro of a roided-out antagonist in the WWE. The heavy bass and deep-voiced screaming destroyed every endorphin that was dancing through my brain. Trendall, one of the other rushees, whose dad was also an Alpha, had a look on his face that turned the drip of paranoia running down my spine into frozen panic.

I followed his eyes up to the balcony and saw a solitary man with a beard that would take me years to achieve. I'd never seen him before, and I thought I had at least *seen* every brother in the house. His medium-height, bulldog-like frame stood in a power position with both hands gripped tightly on the wooden railing, grinding a toothpick between his teeth. His face showed no emotion, like a hairy robot, and he scanned each of us with his eyes like he was doing a head count.

"Who the fuck is that?" I whispered to Monte. He didn't answer.

The bearded man headed for the stairs while I fidgeted and looked for things to stare at besides his menacing face.

He walked slowly up to us wearing a Brooks Brothers button-down that displayed a thick forest of chest hair, khaki shorts with an inseam that would make 1980s Chevy Chase proud, and beach sandals. The chorus of "RE…SPECT" from Pantera's "Walk" sounded through the balcony speakers, and suddenly, with an authoritative leap, the bearded man mounted my table, knocking buckets of ice cream aside as he made his way to the middle.

"Welcome!" he bellowed. "My name is Arthur Weston, but you pieces of shit will address me as Mr. Weston, sir! I am your pledgemaster, and for the foreseeable future, you are FUCKED!"

His stony face, rough beard, and shaggy brown hair showed no sign of weakness. I glanced around the table at faces that had been decorated with total comfort and acceptance just minutes before. Now they wore nothing but somber humility and dejection. Tim had his head down staring into a tub of Blue Bell, and Trendall was visibly shaking as his wide eyes focused on Mr. Weston's hairy feet. We were a bunch of preppy kids from privileged backgrounds who had spent the last few weeks soaring in drunken bliss, and we weren't even close to prepared for a reality check of this magnitude. All the authority figures I'd ever had, including my parents, coaches, and teachers, were much older than me. Mr. Weston was only twenty-one, and was already more intimidating than all of them combined.

"Starting now, you have three minutes to be in the basement, lined up in alphabetical order by last name, with your backs parallel to the wall," he said. "Have your chins in the fucking air, and your eyes on the fucking ceiling."

He had the stage presence of a seasoned general, but even as his tone remained calm I could feel danger, like being in the eye of a great storm. I was frozen. I couldn't move. None of us could.

And that made him angry.

"Now, goddammit! Move your worthless fucking asses!"

He kicked a bucket of Ben & Jerry's into Trendall's face with the accuracy and force of a Cristiano Ronaldo strike. Trendall fell backward off the bench and thudded into the dirt, his nose bleeding and his face covered in vanilla.

"Run, you ice-cream-munching cum stain!" Mr. Weston picked up a second bucket and hurled it at Monte, nailing him in the back and sending him stumbling forward.

I stood up and sprinted aimlessly toward the house, clumsily running into Tim. I realized I had no idea where I was going, while Mr. Weston screamed obscenities.

"Move, you fucking losers! Faster! Run!"

Another bucket of ice cream sailed past my head as Mr. Weston let out a powerful evil laugh. Liquid splattered onto my shoulder and I looked up to see two brothers hanging out of their windows, yelling and throwing beer as we passed.

"Who's smiling now, bitches?" one yelled down at us. "This is a fucking nightmare you'll never wake up from!"

Just like that, rush was over. There would be no more free steak dinners, no more undeserved compliments, and no more getting kidnapped by hot girls with great tits. We were in Mr. Weston's world now, and it was about to get dark.

—————

The moment when pledgeship becomes a reality is gut-wrenching for the rushees. The wool is pulled from their eyes and they realize the fraternity members have been treating them like kings only to enslave them in their pledge program. It's an incredibly sobering moment, and more of a mind-fuck than finding out Santa Claus isn't real...

On the Beginning of Pledgeship

It's all fun and games until somebody gives you a bid. TFM.

The look on the legacy's face when he realizes he's just as fucked as the rest of the pledges. TFM.

The house has that "new pledge class" smell. TFM.

Changing their cell phone contact name prefixes from "Rushee" to "Pledge" and loving every minute of it. TFM.

We had the pledges for under an hour before the risk management chair had to intervene. TFM.

Forcing the pledges to take a moment of silence for their recently deceased dignity. TFM.

"Why are all these guys being so mean?" asked the confused pledge. TFM.

The pledge fire. TFM.

Speed Bump Pledge. TFM.

Wherever it snows, Snow Shovel Pledge goes. TFM.

Mr. Weston's World

IT QUICKLY BECAME OBVIOUS THAT MOST OF US DIDN'T even know the basement existed, much less how to get inside. For a few seconds our directionless pack stalled out until Rogers took the lead. One by one we headed through a heavy wooden door into the dusty, stale dungeon. Once inside, we started yelling our last names at each other in the dark, desperately trying to get in order.

"ADAMS!"

"RUMSEN!"

"TRENDALL! FUCKING TRENDALL!"

"MONTGOMERY!"

"PARSELLS!"

"ROGERS!"

"PRESCOTT!"

I pushed my way in between Parsells and Rogers while the name-yelling continued. It sounded like there was a stampede taking place on the floor above us. Dozens of stomping feet shook the ceiling and sent a cloud of dust pouring down around us. Phil Collins's "In the Air Tonight" had been turned on full blast to smother any cries for help. I stared up at the ceiling and my dad's words echoed in my head. *Take the hazing like a man*. I heard the basement door slam shut. Mr. Weston Sir was among us.

"I want each of you to look at the worthless shitbags to your immediate left and right!" he instructed. "These are your pledge brothers! The men you will suffer with every single day for the next twelve weeks! And you will suffer, you can bet on that."

I looked at Rogers, who looked back at me, and then over at Parsells, who was too afraid to break eye contact with the ceiling.

Mr. Weston shouted again. "Eyes back on the fucking ceiling! You're in my world now, and my world has rules. Pay close attention. My mood depends entirely on whether or not you follow the fucking rules, and my mood is very, very important to you."

He paced back and forth in front of us. Every time he paused I could feel the tension in the room skyrocket. He randomly raised his voice for parts of his delivery he considered especially important.

"These are the rules of pledging...ATTIRE! You will wear a collared polo shirt tucked into Wrangler boot-cut jeans with boots at all times on campus. The only exceptions are TUESDAYS, which are meeting days, when you will wear your PLEDGE UNIFORM, which consists of a white button-down, red tie, and a blue blazer with khaki pants."

He stepped past me and paused for a second to collect his thoughts. The thunderous stomping overhead continued, and dust from the ceiling sprinkled into my eyes. My palms were sweating and I could feel my heartbeat pounding through my chest.

"There will be no hair products, no jewelry, no watches, no ankle socks, no sandals, no facial hair, no hats, no sunglasses, no long hair..."

He hesitated momentarily in front of Parsells, and then yelled directly at him.

"No stupid fucking faces!"

Someone toward the beginning of our alphabetical line sneezed, and Mr. Weston sprung toward him in what seemed like a single bound, defying physics like an NFL linebacker.

"SHUT THE FUCK UP!"

His head was on a swivel as his eyes scanned back and forth, and then he calmed himself and continued. I tried to keep my breathing to a minimum out of fear that I would draw his attention.

"There will be no drinking, no tobacco of any kind, and no drugs. That ice cream was the last fucking treat you'll ever have. You will address every active as 'Mr.,' call him by his last name, and end every sentence with 'sir' when you talk to them. If you see an active on campus you will approach him with a firm handshake and address him like I am about to address this mindless fuck right here."

He stepped in front of Monte and extended one hand firmly for a shake.

"Sir, Alpha pledge Arthur Weston, how are you today, Mr. Montgomery?"

Monte tried to shake his hand without looking at him, but missed awkwardly, and Mr. Weston slapped his hand away.

"Do not fucking touch me! Who the fuck do you think you are?"

He stood on his toes and screamed in Monte's face.

"I will fucking eat you alive! Uncooked! I will fucking eat you!"

He remained on his toes, inches from Monte's face, silent. Monte stood tightlipped and fixed his eyes on the ceiling.

Mr. Weston was looking for a reaction, any excuse to keep demeaning Monte, but he didn't get one and backed away to continue his pacing.

It ended right in front of me.

"Who wants to try and intro me properly?"

Please God, not me.

"You." He poked me in the Adam's apple with his burly index finger. "Address me correctly."

"Sir, Alpha pledge Townes Prescott. How are you today, Mr. Weston, sir?"

"LOUDER, YOU QUIVERING TAINT!"

I could smell the whiskey on his breath.

"Sir, Alpha pledge Townes Prescott, how are you today, Mr. Weston, sir!" I deepened my voice to sound like a badass, but every fluid drop of my testosterone was hiding deep in the tunnels of my ass.

"Fuck you! That's how I'm doing!"

Apparently that was his way of expressing approval, because he moved on.

"You will change your cell phone voice mail to 'Alpha pledge, *your full name*, please leave a message.' You're not to use bikes, buses, or any other form of transportation such as skateboards or Rollerblades. If I see you on a skateboard I will put it inside you fucking sideways and you will never see the inside of this house again! You will WALK to class. No god-damn music, and no goddamn Facebook. If one of you cock-suckers writes on my wall I will 'poke' you in the throat with my fucking knee. Delete your account."

He paused and spit a giant loogie, seemingly disgusted that his one-sided conversation with us wasn't over.

"You will respect all ladies, even heifers and handicaps, and you will never use the front door of the fraternity house. You use the back door, the asshole of the house, because you are SHIT!"

In my peripheral vision I could see him looking up and down the line to catch one of us even thinking about smiling. The room was still filled with the booming, disorienting echo of stomping on the floor above us.

"Does everyone understand the rules?" Mr. Weston asked.

Not a single one of us spoke, terrified that one of the rules we'd already forgotten was to never respond to a question.

"I said, does everyone understand the fucking rules? The answer is sir yes sir!"

"Sir yes sir!" we rang out in unison.

"Louder!"

"SIR YES SIR!" The volume of our response shook the room.

"Fucking pathetic," he said, but his gruff tone gave off a sense of pride.

Then he swung the basement door open into the wall, deepening the already existing doorknob-sized hole, and was gone as quickly as he came. We stood in silence, staring up at the ceiling.

Are we supposed to leave? I had no fucking idea.

The music suddenly cut off in the middle of a drum solo, and the stomping above us ceased. I heard the last few steps of Mr. Weston's heavy feet ascending the staircase, and each one made me feel a little bit safer. When his footsteps stopped we were alone in silence for minutes that seemed like days. I checked down the line to my left and right, making sure I wasn't the only idiot still staring fearfully at the ceiling. Then I imagined the world outside the basement. I saw kids in their dorms studying for exams that were weeks away; my parents at home enjoying dinner by the fire; tiny Asian women in a Malaysian sweatshop sewing shoes. So many happy, blissfully ignorant lives. Maybe they were the lucky ones for not being conned into this ridiculous world of tyranny.

Suddenly the speaker system kicked back on and Dean Martin's "Ain't That a Kick in the Head" was blaring through the house, accompanied by the clatter of dozens of feet running above us and down the stairs outside. The door swung back open and Atwater sprinted through with a bottle of champagne, spraying down the line as he ran past. Dozens of other actives followed, all holding champagne bottles, dousing us and jumping around like fucking maniacs. They filed into the basement until the room was filled.

"All right, you sons of bitches!" yelled Atwater. "Tonight is your fucking bid night! Your final night of freedom!"

The actives erupted as I forced myself to continue staring at the ceiling. My mind was being fucked so hard that it actually hurt, like a brain freeze. The champagne burned my eyes as I was strapped into the emotional roller coaster.

"You don't have to stare at the ceiling anymore," said Atwater as he pressed a bottle of champagne to my chest. "Tonight is a fucking celebration!"

I grabbed the bottle but held it without taking a sip, worried that I was being set up. I glanced around and saw that all my pledge brothers were being handed bottles as well. Atwater laughed at my distrust and stepped back to address the line.

"It is extremely important that you remember everything your pledge trainer Mr. Weston said here tonight, but the rest of the evening you should have the motherfucking time of your lives! Tomorrow morning you will be nothing more than shitty pledge scum, but tonight you are celebrating the fact that you and your pledge brothers are pledge scum for the best fucking fraternity on this campus."

The actives shuffled around congratulating us, shaking our hands, and delivering quips to commemorate our accomplishment. Some were friendlier than others.

"Congratulations, man. Tonight is going to be insane."

"Good job, bro. Let's get fucking sloppy."

"Enjoy tonight, you fucking pledge turd. Tomorrow the shit begins."

Monte shrugged his shoulders in an act of mental capitulation. Trendall upended his bottle to drown his anxiety. Then Atwater spoke up again.

"Let's head upstairs and get this shit started! The girls will be here soon."

———

If he is any good at his job, your pledge trainer will haunt you from the moment he introduces himself until the day you die. He is the man in charge of every hazing session you go through. He orchestrates the entirety of your education about the fraternity, and bonds your pledge class by breaking you down and then building you back up together as one. But even after initiation, he never really becomes just another one of the guys. He's always your pledge trainer...

On Pledge Trainers

Pledgeship was four years ago, but I still hold my breath and look around for my pledge trainer whenever I hear the intro to "Walk" by Pantera. TFM.

Unanimous vote for the marine as pledge trainer. TFM.

Even the active chapter is starting to buy into the pledge trainer's mind-fuck. TFM.

Congratulations, we just elected the white Ray Lewis as pledge trainer. TFM.

Pledge trainer gave the pledges the hazing hotline number. Little do they know, it's our drunkest active's cell phone number. Welcome to hell boys. TFM.

Mid-chapter meeting haze off to decide on the next pledge trainer. TFM.

Parking a pledge's car for him. TFM.

"Do it, pledge. DO IT NOW!" TFM.

The Final Night of Freedom

I GASPED FOR CLEAN AIR AS ATWATER USHERED US OUT of the musty basement like traumatized cattle. Mr. Weston's voice was still echoing violently through my head as I tried to make sense of what was happening. The sort of confusion that can only be created by the perfect mind-fuck was still visible on many of my pledge brothers' faces. The expression on my face was similar to that of an escaped mental patient getting a blowjob during a root canal. I was relieved that I had gotten my bid, horrified that Mr. Weston existed, pumped about the party, and dreading the beginning of pledgeship the next day.

The actives had reassumed control of the porch, and there was no fucking way I was going to be the first moron to stroll up and pretend we were all best friends again, so I stood my ground and waited to see how everything played out. But nobody else made a move.

"Why the fuck are you just standing there?" asked Atwater, pointing to the stairs. "Go! Party!"

"Is Mr. Weston up there?" asked Tim.

"No, you won't see him for the rest of the night."

Tim turned and bounded up the stairs with his bottle of

champagne. I took a swig to get the taste of the basement out of my mouth and followed him.

We were greeted by a mob of actives and the crowd immediately swallowed Tim. David Young, one of the seniors I had met at a dinner, put his arm around me and pulled me in.

"Y'all are solid," he hiccuped. "Solid pledge class. You'll do just fine." Then he let go and turned back for the next guy, breath reeking of Budweiser and chewing tobacco, and I heard him say the same thing verbatim.

With every step I was stopped and given more words of approval and congratulations. When I finally got through the welcome committee I turned to find Monte and noticed a pack of Jeeps, Tahoes, and trucks parking in the street. Sorority girls were jumping out, screaming and hugging. It had been a full week since the ones going through rush had hung out with us because of their "sorority silence," where freshmen weren't allowed to talk to guys or drink as part of their recruitment process. The yard filled up as more and more of them arrived, and then they made their way toward the house. They were all wearing tank tops with their letters shaped by rhinestones, along with neon face paint and temporary tattoos.

Monte walked up and nodded to me.

"Thank God," he said, looking at the girls. "I was really starting to miss them."

We clinked our bottles together and I sloshed back the little champagne I had left and hurled the empty bottle at the roof of the Sigma house next door. While I watched it sail through the air I felt the back of my shirt tighten and a hand grip my shoulder.

"What the *fuck* are you doing, pledge?"

I turned around to face a pair of bushy eyebrows on a head covered in shaggy brown hair belonging to a guy wearing an untucked dark green polo and a look of disgust. I struggled to get my words out.

"I was just—"

"Is that how you talk to an active? Why the fuck do you want to be in this fraternity? Who are you? Why do you deserve to be my brother? Why are you even here?"

He was in attack mode, rattling off rhetorical questions in an angry tirade. Any response would've just fueled the flame, so I decided maintaining eye contact and looking intimidated was the safest play.

"What are you, fucking stupid or something?" he continued.

Atwater slid out from between two girls and grabbed him.

"Goddammit, Jackson, you fucking jackass, save it for tomorrow."

"What's the big deal?" Jackson smiled at him. "I was just having a little fun with the kid." He smirked at me and chugged his beer as he turned away.

"Ignore that," said Atwater as we both watched Jackson push past Trendall. "Did you see how many fucking girls I got for you?"

"Yeah, I just saw an army of them pull up. I'm assuming sorority silence is over?"

"You're damn right. Get in there and make me proud."

He turned to help two actives carrying a Gatorade water cooler. Pink liquid sloshed out as they set it down on a bench, and Scott McCandles threw a bag of 250 red Solo cups down next to it. Atwater grabbed a cup and threw it to me.

"Might as well," he said.

I headed for the cooler and Monte trailed me, trying to reason with me as I filled up my first cup.

"Whoa! Do you really want to end up like Tim after Paint Your Toga? That shit is lethal."

I nodded and gulped down the pink mixture. "I don't give a shit, dude. I'm getting David Hasselhoff drunk tonight."

The rest of our pledge brothers worked their way through the gauntlet, and the actives faded into the house after growing tired of congratulations. Trendall bounced in and out of groups, redirecting each conversation to Mr. Weston in a lowered voice until he was shooed away by those who were trying to stay positive and hit on girls. I was waiting in line for the cooler and well on my way to brutally murdering all my brain cells when I heard a familiar voice.

"Isn't that punch supposed to be for girls?" It was Allison. I hadn't seen her since the incident with the cannon.

"Well...girls and real degenerates who like blacking out immediately."

She went in for a hug, but the punch had already begun to grab hold of my conscience, so I went in for an early, probably inappropriate makeout. She turned her head and giggled.

"Oh no, sweetheart." She smirked. "We had fun, but I'm a little too old for you and you're a little too crazy for me. You need a girl in your age group." She grabbed a shorter girl with long blonde hair by the shoulder and turned her toward me. "This is Amy. She's one of our new girls."

I immediately refocused my efforts. "Amy, I'm Townes. Nice to meet you."

She smiled and rocked her shoulders back and forth.

"You want some punch?" I offered like a true gentleman.

"Sure," she said. "We're celebrating, aren't we?"

"I'll leave you two to talk," Allison said, and winked at me before walking away.

For the next thirty minutes Amy schooled me on sorority recruitment and how excited she was while I tried to appropriately divide my attention between her and getting dumbface wasted. The difference between sorority and fraternity bid day became clear immediately.

"Oh my God, I like absolutely love my new sisters! They are all so gorgeous and sweet!"

"Definitely." I smiled. "Congratulations."

"I mean like, being a Pi, it's the best thing that's ever happened to me. Ya know? They just keep giving us presents! You must be so excited to be an Alpha. Did you get any presents?"

"Uh—not yet. How many girls are in your pledge class?"

"Like sixty-three of the absolute prettiest most gorgeous girls ever. I mean obvi some of them are going to other houses tonight too, but at least like twenty of us will be here all night."

The actives were keeping to themselves inside with the older girls while we mingled with the new members of various sororities on the porch. Monte returned and I introduced him to Amy. Then she took us around and introduced us to some of her pledge sisters, all of whom were total fucking smokeshows. More and more girls kept arriving and the ratio became increasingly favorable. There were forty-two of us and twice as many of them.

After discussing the football schedule with the girls I was nine cups of punch deep, well on my way to blacking out, and smiling like a circus clown with red stains on and around my lips. The sound system on the back deck was playing country classics as my new pledge brothers and I started belligerently bonding, arm in arm with some of the Pi girls, singing along to "Friends in Low Places." The actives weren't fucking with us, Mr. Weston was nowhere to be seen, and I didn't have a worry in the world.

As the song ended, five older girls came skipping from inside wielding handles of Taaka vodka, which is the equivalent of bottled homeless urine. They worked their way through a group of us, pulling heads back and dumping vodka down unsuspecting throats.

Tim walked up with his arm around a redhead. He leaned in toward me, attempting to be discreet.

"I'm taking her to do some X in the bathroom." He laughed, but I knew he wasn't kidding.

"Seriously? Now?" I asked.

"You want in?"

One of the Taaka girls walked up and gave me the "tilt your head back" look that I had become familiar with. I took a mouthful and swallowed as fast as I could before answering Tim.

"I'm good with this shit, but thanks."

"Your loss, pussy." He stumbled off with the ginger.

"What are they doing?" asked Amy, who clearly half heard our conversation. "That's my pledge sister Whitney!"

"Nothing, nothing. She has to pee. He's taking her to the bathroom."

Amy was telling me about how she did cheer in high school and considered doing the same in college when Atwater walked out with his eyes completely glazed over.

"Inside to fuck shit up!" he yelled. "Everybody in!"

I wasn't exactly jumping at the chance to rejoin the actives, but Amy grabbed my hand and we headed for the door. On our way down the hallway toward the party we passed Tim's redhead coming out of the bathroom. Tim emerged thirty seconds later, looked furtively to his left and right, and cut to the front of the mob to find Whitney again.

"Your friend is weird," Amy yelled over the music.

"He's a good guy," I assured her. "He'll take good care of her."

When we made our way into the party room I decided to switch to beer for safety's sake, and headed for the tub with Amy attached to my hand. It was filled with ice and packed to the brim with Natty Light and Keystone.

"You want one?" I asked Amy as I submerged my hand.

"I'm fine with punch, thanks, sweetie."

More for sweetie.

I looked to the front of the room and saw a snowball of destruction beginning to form. The actives started flipping trash cans, throwing half-full beers at each other, and pouring entire cans onto each other's heads. A wooden chair flew through the air into the wall, breaking into pieces. I realized they were trashing the place because now they had us to clean it all up for them. Even at our own bid night party, they were making sure we'd pay for it tomorrow.

Amy headed in for the less destructive portion of the crowd as I cracked my beer, held it a foot above my face, and let it splash into my mouth. I lost sight of her when a roll of toilet paper flew over my head, unraveling onto my shoulder, and she mixed in with the hundreds of people dancing. As I made my way forward to find her I spotted a shirtless Nate, ignoring song lyrics and screaming at the top of his lungs as if the apocalypse was imminent.

"Nate!" I yelled to get his attention.

He turned toward me, poured his beer onto my head, yelling the entire time, and ran off toward the tub for another. As liquid ran down my face someone pushed me hard from behind and sent me stumbling forward. I turned around and faced Jackson. His shirt was ripped and his hair was soaked. He looked like a bad celebrity mug shot.

"I fucking hate you," he said, letting out a breath-filled laugh and then walking away shaking his head.

Deep bass was pounding through the floor, freeing girls from their inhibitions with every beat. They moved with the music in lines of three or four, spread throughout the dance floor. Some were facing each other and grinding, while others were ass to ass. Suddenly a random chick grabbed me by the arm and pulled me into her group. I had two girls behind me and two in front, all holding drinks overhead, but none of them were Amy. Tim came out of nowhere with Whitney and attached himself to her backside, and they became the caboose to the slutty dancing train. The X had obviously kicked in, and Tim was dancing with more ferocity than all the girls combined, aggressively attacking Whitney with his pelvis. She didn't even seem to notice, just danced with her eyes closed and smiled like she was the only one in the room.

The song changed and triggered the girl in front of me to repeatedly drop her ass to the floor and then pop it back up, rubbing it into my crotch like she was trying to get me to precum my fucking khakis. It took all my focus not to pop a raging boner, and all I could do was stand there and drink while she made me into a human stripper pole. Tim was leaning back with his chin to his chest, staring shamelessly at Whitney's ass with both hands clenched high in the air like he just won gold at the Olympics.

When the song ended my crotch masseuse turned around and smiled at me. She was a solid 5. I bailed immediately toward the back porch to try to find Amy.

The party had continued to grow while my dick was being

assaulted, and the back porch was filled to the railing with people as well. I was getting to the point of absolute sloppiness, but this was my fucking bid night. It was supposed to be the drunkest night of my life, and I needed to step it up another notch. I spotted a few guys ripping cigs and decided that getting some nicotine in my blood might help. I walked up and asked one of my pledge brothers, Ryan Penny, if I could bum one.

"Yeah, no problem," he said. "You don't mind Marlboro Reds, do you?"

"No, I don't fucking mind, Penny. Do I look like a commie?"

I took my first drag and tried to it play off when I immediately felt my knees go weak. Monte stumbled out of the house with Nate, smiling and holding the bottom of his shirt up as a basket to transport six beers. Nate, still shirtless and covered in sweat, pulled two from each of his pockets.

"We're shotgunning these fuckers!" Nate ordered.

Penny grabbed a beer, pulled a knife from his boot, whipped it open, and stabbed a hole in the can in one fluid motion. Then he passed the knife to me, and around it went. Eight of us circled up, and Nate made a toast.

"To this semester, and our pledge class. I love you guys, and just remember, no matter what these insane bastards put us through over the next twelve weeks, we're going to come out alive on the other side and run this fucking campus!"

We all yelled in agreement and popped our cans. Monte finished first and dropped his can at his feet, letting the remaining foam run onto the deck.

"First, motherfuckers!" he celebrated. "I'm going in for more. We're doing another round."

The rest of us slammed our cans as he took off into the house. Suddenly the Taaka girls, who clearly had just watched us shotgun our beers, were huddled around the eight of us.

"Open up, boys!"

These booze sirens had some sort of inexplicable control over us, so we all tilted our heads back and waited to be served. The girl who approached me was a tall blonde wearing a low-cut halter top, and when she smiled I had no choice but to make a run at her.

"I'm Townes. What's your name?"

"My name is I'm dating a senior in Alpha."

I tilted my head back and opened my mouth immediately.

She poured until I couldn't swallow anymore, and then kept pouring until I spit up vodka all over Penny's back.

"What the fuck?" Penny turned around, confused.

The alleged girlfriend laughed as she turned to walk back inside. I couldn't tell if she was fucking with me, or the active she was dating had sent her out as bait knowing one of us would hit on her and be subject to pledge punishment.

That last vodka "shot" took me from shitfaced to out-of-control-I-need-to-be-put-to-bed drunk. As I felt my mouth oversalivating, Monte reemerged with another shirt full of beers.

"All right, let's go again!" he said.

"Damn it, Monte, you just avoided the fucking Taaka girls, you prick," Nate scolded him.

"Actually, they got me on my way out, so stop bitching and do another shotgun."

That put Nate in his place and he grabbed for Penny's knife.

Tim gave the toast this time. I didn't really hear what he was saying because I was busy trying to mentally ready my stomach for another full beer, but it was something about America and the bald eagle and how Kennedy was right about the Russians. Then he counted to three and we pounded our beers. I finished a little over half before dropping the can and rushing to the edge of the balcony. Pink vomit launched from my stomach through my mouth. The guys were all very amused.

"You all right, you fucking lightweight?" Tim asked as he kicked me in the ass while I was still leaning over the edge.

"I'm fine, just got an air bubble."

I checked my phone as I wiped my mouth. It was nearly 1 a.m. and I had three texts from Allison.

Allison: *Where areeyou? KT is lookjng for u. near the spearkers.*

Allison: *Quitbeingafuckass holec*

Allison: *UGGGGGHHHHHH*

I stumbled back inside and grabbed a beer out of the first tub I saw to freshen my breath. The party was still in full swing and all the guys split up to try to spend our final night of freedom with a female companion. I headed toward the dance floor and found Amy making one of the four-foot-tall speakers her dance partner while Allison and her other sisters watched, laughed, and filmed her with their iPhones.

"TOWNES!" Amy screamed immediately and jumped on me. "*Wheeeere* have you beeeeen?"

"I was outside with the guys," I said, trying not to breathe my throw-up breath on her. "You doing okay?"

"I'm fiiiiiiine!" She was using about six extra vowels for each word. "Here!" She handed me her cup of punch. "I don't want this."

"And she definitely doesn't need it," added Allison. "Get

her out of here. She lives on the eighth floor of Manor. Don't you live in Manor?" She winked at me again. It made my dick twitch every time.

As weird as it was to have a girl that I had recently been inside of, and totally would've fucked to completion had it not been for an ill-timed cannon explosion, now hooking me up with a younger sister of hers, there was no way I was passing it up.

"Let's get you home," I told Amy.

Amy wrapped her arm in mine and Allison slapped me on the ass as we walked away. We were passing through the ass-hole of the house when Amy caught her sandal on the door-step and fell forward face first to the deck. I pulled her to her feet while she giggled. There was no way this girl was going to successfully walk all the way back to our dorm.

"Where are you two lovebirds going?" Monte asked as he walked out behind us.

"I'm trying to get Amy here back safely to Manor, but she can't walk and I definitely can't fucking drive."

"Fuck it, I need to get home and call Sarah anyway," said Monte. "I'll drive y'all."

I tossed him my keys before he could change his mind, threw Amy over my shoulder, and headed to my truck.

Monte drove 20 mph the entire way home like an elderly woman with cataracts, but we made it. When we got to the elevator I pressed 8, and Amy spoke for the first time since we left the house.

"No no no no no I don't want to go to bed yet. Can't I hang out with youuuuuu?"

"With me?" I said, surprised. "Sure you can."

I hadn't pegged her for the type, and definitely didn't think she'd be awake much longer, but this was a definite hookup move by her. Monte was making blowjob hand gestures behind her.

"Absolutely, Amy," he said. "You're more than welcome to hang in our room."

When we hit our floor Monte dialed Sarah's number.

"I'll talk to Sarah in the hall," he said behind Amy's back. "I'll give you an hour."

"Tell her I love her," I said sarcastically.

"I love you too," Amy chimed in.

I wasn't sure if she was talking to me, so I just ignored the misunderstanding.

When I unlocked the door and hit the lights, Amy pushed past me giggling and flopped down on my bed.

"Come here," she said sweetly.

I turned the light back off and made my approach. We made out for a few minutes, and then I remembered that I'd thrown up less than an hour ago and pulled away.

"What's wrong?" she asked.

"Nothing, nothing, sorry."

"Am I not good?"

"Good at making out? I was just thinking about how ridiculous that party was."

"I can make you think about something else. Lay down under the covers and take off your shorts."

I ripped away the covers and pulled my shorts off like they were on fire. She climbed on top of me fully clothed and pulled the covers over us.

"Try thinking about this." She peeled off her shirt to reveal a pink-laced bra, and then pulled my boxers down to my ankles.

Thirty seconds of sucking later and I was still as soft as a wet, uncooked hot dog. This couldn't even be classified as "whiskey dick." More like in-order-for-your-vital-organs-to-function-we-have-to-shut-down-everything-else dick. I closed my eyes and desperately tried to imagine Victoria's Secret models' tits bouncing down the runway, but instead I got the spins. Amy must have been too drunk to notice, because she went right on working on my windsock like a champ. The only sound in the room was the *squelsh squelsh squelsh* of her fruitless efforts.

I decided there was no reason for both of us to go unsatisfied and flipped her around on her back. As I was kissing down her stomach I looked up into her eyes, and we both knew where I was going.

"Do it," she said as she raised her hips slightly. "Do me with your tongue."

I dove in and used my tongue as a weapon in the swordfight against her vagina. She immediately let out a moan and wrapped her legs around my head, squirming and gripping my hair with both hands like she was controlling me with dual joysticks.

"Yes yes yes yes," she whispered. "Right there, don't stop."

I was licking like a lizard that hasn't had a drink in months and just discovered a pool of delicious water. Every thirty seconds or so I tried to change my approach and work in some finger action.

Finally she let out a long, satisfied sigh and pulled me up by my hair to kiss me. I crammed myself up against the wall next to her in my tiny bed as she rested one arm on my chest and closed her eyes.

"I'm tired." She yawned. "I'm sleeping here."

"I thought that was a given," I said. "Good night, Amy."

"Night night, Townes."

I closed my eyes and fell asleep almost instantly.

The next morning I woke up on my back with my boxers still around my ankles, and, ironically, a raging case of morning wood. Amy was gone, and Monte was still asleep in his bed.

"Monte!" I yelled to wake him.

He rolled over and barely opened his eyes.

"Jesus, what?"

"Were you awake for that?" I asked.

"Was I awake for what? I passed the fuck out on a couch in the hallway and when I came in around 4 a.m. you guys were out cold. You better have fucked her."

"Dude, I wish. Way too much punch. I ended up tongue deep for like thirty minutes."

"It happens. Now leave me alone, we've got one more hour to sleep before we have to go to house cleanup."

Just thinking about how Mr. Weston was waiting for us at the absolutely trashed house made it impossible to fall back asleep, so I took a bottle of water from the fridge and grabbed my laptop. As I looked through Facebook pictures of the guys and me covered in paint at the Alpha house it suddenly became real that rush was over. I scrolled over and clicked "Deactivate your account" as Mr. Weston had demanded, and then closed my laptop and tried to ready myself to face pledgeship head-on.

————

Bid night is one of the most celebrated nights in Greek culture. For the actives it's the end of having to convince a bunch of younger guys that joining the fraternity is the best decision they'll ever make. For the rushees it's the beginning of a whole new life in the fraternity with a whole new group of best friends in their pledge class. It's also their last chance to get as blackout drunk as they can before the rough stuff starts...

On Bid Night, Getting Fucked Up, and Fucking Shit Up

Give that guy two bids, cause he'll probably lose one tonight. TFM.

Alcohol is only a depressant if your life sucks. TFM.

Drinking away problems you don't have. TFM.

What I do when I'm blacked out is none of my damn business. TFM.

Getting "light the wrong end of your cigarette" drunk. TFM.

The "No Alcohol Beyond This Point" sign might as well say, "I bet you can't chug that whole drink." TFM.

The door that got kicked in last night was a beer pong table this afternoon. TFM.

Proving the "beer before liquor, never been sicker" phrase is complete horseshit on a daily basis. TFM.

There's a fine line between confident and cocky, and I just snorted it. TFM.

Losing a pledge on bid night. Like actually losing him. Seriously, he's still missing. TFM.

The correct way to use a pool. TFM.

Flipping tables for fucking fun. TFM.

"I'm not picking this shit up. Call the pledges." TFM.

"That door was old anyway." TFM.

The Hazement

NORMAL STUDENTS HAVE NIGHTMARES ABOUT GIVING a speech naked in front of a packed classroom, or sleeping through a final exam. After our first lineup I had a nightmare where I was walking through campus wearing cargo shorts and an Affliction tee. Everyone I passed was pointing and laughing. I woke up, startled, when Mr. Weston jumped out from behind a tree with blood smeared down his face and a paddle in his hand. Every morning the first thought that popped into my mind was *Fuck, I'm still a pledge.* Each day brought a different set of completely pain-in-the-ass tasks, like getting eight orders of chicken fingers for two stoned actives, fighting like gladiators in the sand volleyball pit for their amusement, or washing one of their trucks until he could see the pubes on his nut sack in the reflection. (Really, I had to sit there and watch him check.) Every time my phone rang I knew it was another active with another chore, and we were on call 24/7.

No matter how hard we worked, there was no reward. Two weeks in, Monte and I dusted, swept, and mopped a five-bedroom house for two hours. When we finished, the seniors who lived there let their black Lab inside completely covered in mud, and chased him through the house, splattering filth all over the floors. Then they made us clean the entire place again. Every Tuesday night at 11 p.m. we had "pledge meetings" in the basement, which consisted of reciting everything we'd learned from the pledge handbook, and paying dearly for any mistakes our pledge class had made that week. Those lineups were the easy ones, because we knew they were coming. If one of us made a mistake that Mr. Weston felt deserved immediate punishment, he could call a surprise lineup at any time. Unfortunately, when you're a pledge, literally every fucking thing you do is a mistake, and Mr. Weston loved surprise lineups. We ended up having at least three a week.

One fateful Thursday I found out what it felt like to be responsible for such a lineup. I was on the way to my 1 p.m. economics class when I was stopped by an Alpha.

"You're one of our pledges, right?" he asked.

I knew he was an Alpha because of the 2007 rush T-shirt he was wearing, but he was obviously one of the older guys who didn't come around much anymore. I would've remembered seeing him because he was six foot five with a barrel chest and veins popping out of the receding hairline on his forehead. I held out my hand to intro him.

"Sir, Alpha pledge Prescott. How are you today, Mr., um . . . I'm sorry, sir, I don't recall your last name."

He gripped my hand tightly, smiled, and said, "Not as fucking sorry as you're gonna be." Then he walked away.

That night at 9 p.m. when I was studying finance in my room I got a call from Mr. Weston.

"Eleven o'clock meeting tonight in full pledge uniform at the house." *Click.* Fuck.

Before every lineup the forty-two of us would meet in the parking lot to get in alphabetical order and jog into the house, where we'd receive our instructions. The mood was never cheery, and that night was no different, except that we could see Mr. Weston waiting for us outside on the balcony. As we made our way toward the staircase he started barking orders.

"Don't even fucking come up here. Get into the basement, get into your spots, and get ready to have your fucking nuts cut and handed to you."

No matter how many times we were sent to the basement, there was no getting used to it. Broken glass and bottle caps were strewn about the floor, which was comprised of hundred-year-old dirt, dust, and grime. The thick air carried the permanent scent of foul body odor. In one corner was a decrepit couch that was definitely older than me, and in another was half of a foosball table that had been in a fire at some point. There were generations of junk down there, but no windows, no lights, and no escape. From the first time I was introduced to the basement on bid night until I take my last breath, it will be a horrifying danger zone that signifies mental incapacitation.

I shuffled through the door and up against the wall with the rest of my pledge brothers, raised my chin to the sky, and glued my eyeballs to the ceiling. I heard several sets of feet making their way down the stairs toward us, and quickly made sure my tie was straight.

During a lineup, it was best not to draw attention to yourself. The less you are singled out, the better. This seems a simple task when there are forty-one other pledges shoulder to shoulder against the wall wearing the same uniform, from blazers to boat shoes, but it's not.

I looked one last time to my left and right to make sure I was between Parsells and Rogers, and then stared up at the ceiling, trying to maintain composure as Mr. Weston and three others stomped into our midst. They slammed the door behind them, and I lost focus and glanced over at them. Big mistake. One of the cronies, Mr. Harris, locked eyes with me and sprung into action.

Classic Hazing Tactic #1: If a pledge makes eye contact with you, tell him to stop eye-fucking you and shame him without remorse.

"Did you just eye-fuck me, pledge?" asked Mr. Harris.

He got right in my face like an angry MLB coach would to an umpire who just made the worst call of all time.

"No sir, Mr. Harris, sir," I quickly responded.

His breath stunk like bourbon, and he slammed both hands into the wall on either side of my head.

"This kid thinks he can look me in the eye. Look at me again, you sackless son of a bitch! Do it again!"

I focused on one of the support beams on the ceiling and kept my face as straight as possible to hide my fear. He lowered his voice.

"Don't you ever, ever undress me with your eyes again, you horny little fuck."

The beauty of these hazing sessions is that they often become hilarious, whether intentional or not. Even during the darkest of times, some of the more creative insults make it hard not to crack a smile, and if you smile everyone pays. I bit my tongue to fight off a grin while Mr. Weston addressed us.

"Since your pledge brother here is missing a chromosome, everyone take off your jackets and get on bows and toes NOW!"

I took off my blazer and dropped to the ground instantly. The four of them started pulling beer bottle caps from their pockets and tossing them to the floor around us. Mr. Stevens, a five-foot-five sophomore with the beer gut of a senior, threw two bottle caps at me and bent down to bark in my face.

"You better have those fucking bottle caps under your elbows, Prescott!"

The bows-and-toes position is similar to push-up position, except you put your elbows on the ground instead of your hands. This becomes really fucking painful after a while, and the pain is obviously worse with bottle caps cutting into your elbows.

I scrambled, quickly sliding one bottle cap under each elbow. As I was adjusting to lessen the pain, Mr. Harris's boots stomped to a halt in front of me.

"Not you, dumbass." He yanked me up by my shirt and slammed me back against the wall. "You're going to watch."

Classic Hazing Tactic #2: Make the guy who screwed up feel guilty by having the rest of the pledge class suffer from his mistake.

Mr. Harris grabbed me by the back of my button-down and shoved me around the room.

"Tell all of your pledge brothers what you did!"

I had no idea what he meant.

"Sir?"

"Tell them! Tell them how you fucked them!"

"Sir, I eye-fucked you, sir," I responded.

"Not me, you idiot!" he yelled. "God, you're a fucking moron. I want you to get down and say, 'I fucked you' to each of your pledge brothers."

He dragged me directly over to Adams, the first person in line, who was already shaking from the pain in his elbows.

"Tell him!" Mr. Harris demanded.

I knelt down and said, "I fucked you" to the back of his head.

"Louder!"

"I FUCKED YOU!"

Controlling me like a puppet by the back of my shirt, he led me around the room and forced me to tell all forty-one of my pledge brothers.

"I fucked you!"

He pulled me to the next person.

"I fucked you!"

I had to say it so many times that I started to genuinely believe that I had permanently fucked each of them; that everything that had ever happened to them was my fault; that when they died as old men in their beds, right before they took their last breath they'd gasp, "Prescott fucked me."

"Do you like that?" Mr. Weston asked the group. "Do you like the way Pledge Prescott fucks you? You guys are the worst fucking pledge class in the history of this fraternity."

Classic Hazing Tactic #3: Telling every single pledge class that they are the worst pledge class you've ever had.

I stood there, panting and looking at the suffering my stupidity had caused, and then Mr. Harris grabbed me by the shoulders and threw me back toward my spot.

I stumbled back against the wall and looked up at the ceiling, and suddenly all four drunken ball-hazers were slurring obscenities in my face. Their flurry of insults ran together.

"You fucking shit-stick I swear to God..."

"...schoolgirl fucking jerkoff jizz rag..."

"...miniature donkey fuck doll!"

Finally, over the shouting, I was able to decipher Mr. Weston giving me a chance at redemption to save my friends.

"Give me the alphabet back-to-back without fucking up!"

He was referring to the Greek alphabet, which we all had to memorize our first week of pledgeship. We weren't just expected to know it; we were expected to be able to recite it at the speed of a cocaine-fueled auctioneer.

"Sir! Alpha-Beta-Gamma-Delta-Epsilon-Zeta-Eta-Theta-Iota-Kappa-Lambda-Mu-Nu-Xi-Omicron-Pi-Rho-Sigma-Tau-Upsilon-Phi-Chi-Psi-Omega!"

Pure adrenaline to save my pledge brothers from permanent elbow scarring had gifted me with a momentarily blazing intellect. Just when I was about to give birth to one happy thought, Mr. Weston violently aborted it.

"Where the *fuck* was my sir sandwich, Prescott?"

I had only given him one slice of bread.

"I don't want a poor man's hot dog bun! Again!" he demanded.

"Sir! Alpha-Beta-Gamma-Delta-Epsilon-Zeta-Eta-Theta-Iota-Kappa-Lambda-Mu-Nu-Xi-Omicron-Pi-Rho-Sigma...uh... Sigma—"

"Stop!" Mr. Weston barked. I tried to continue: "Sigma, uh...Tau..."

"Shut that fucking hole in your face!" Mr. Stevens shoved me in the chest.

I was crestfallen. My friends were emitting loud grunts of pain and wobbling on their elbows as the muscles in their arms grew tired. Mr. Weston's intuitive senses kicked in and he decided to switch up his twisted game plan of pain before any real injury occurred.

"Everybody up!" he yelled. "Your pledge brother Prescott here doesn't care enough about you to save you. Get back up against the wall and tune the goddamn TV!"

Tuning the TV consists of squatting, knees bent at a ninety-degree angle, with your hands out in front of you moving back and forth as if you're tuning an old-timey television. At first it's a welcome change of pace to bows and toes, but in time it wears you down as your thighs start to burn. I hit the wall and Mr. Harris squatted in front of me, yelling up into my face.

"What am I watching, pledge? What the fuck am I watching?"

"Sir, uh, you're watching Cinemax, sir!"

"Why the fuck would I watch Skinemax, pledge? Do you think I have to slap my own ham? That's what your little sister is for."

For a second I forgot that I don't have a sister, and felt a great wave of depression come over me as I imagined Mr. Harris angrily pounding the innocence out of her nonexistent body. I tried for a better answer.

"Sir, you're watching *SportsCenter*, sir!"

He threw his hands up in disgust and walked away. I kept rotating my hands as fast as I possibly could while my thighs ached, but another thirty seconds passed and I still wasn't being verbally assaulted. The actives had grown silent.

The booming sound of a single pair of boots echoed through the room. Someone was coming down the stairs toward us.

"Holy shit, now you're all really fucked!" said Mr. Harris in an almost reverent manner.

"They're so fucked," said Mr. Stevens.

"Fucking fucked!" said Mr. Weston with more joy than I'd ever heard him express.

Classic Hazing Tactic #4: Constantly remind the pledges that they are, in fact, fucked.

"Everybody back against the wall! Line the fuck up!" Mr. Weston yelled.

I fixed my eyes on the ceiling, and step by step the pair of heavy boots descended the stairs. The room went completely silent as he walked down the line. He didn't say a word, and I didn't have the slightest clue what we were dealing with.

I heard the distinct sound of a zipper being unzipped. Mr. Harris started laughing. The splattering of piss on the dirt between Rogers's legs made me cringe, and the laughter of all five actives filled the room. I felt urine splattering onto my boat shoes, but kept my eyes on the ceiling. His stream splashed with abnormal power against the hard ground. He just stood there, breathing hard with relief, and pissed, and pissed, and pissed.

When the stream finally became a trickle, Mr. Weston stifled his laughter and delivered the bad news.

"Looks like you boys have been blessed with a visit from The Maglite."

I had heard rumors of The Maglite during rush. He was a sixth-year senior on his second victory lap whose schedule was comprised of nonstop binge drinking and inhaling rails of blow as long as his fourteen-inch penis. The Maglite avoided graduation like the plague so he could continue jackhammering freshman girls with his God-given endowment. The guy was a fucking legend, but I had never met him. None of us had. It was at that moment, staring at the ceiling while I stood in my piss-filled loafers, that I realized he was the unknown

Alpha I'd run into on campus. My heart rate ascended to an uncharted new level, and for a second I thought I was going to collapse.

He reeked of whiskey and cigar smoke, and the mix of his stench and piss filled my nostrils. He zipped his pants back up and took two steps, positioning himself directly in front of me.

"Take off your goddamn shoes," he demanded, speaking slowly with a southern drawl.

I bent down, slipped off one shoe and then the other, and heard the unrolling of duct tape. It sent chills down my spine. The Maglite hit me in the chest with two unopened cans of Grizzly Wintergreen dip.

"Pack every fucking grain of dip from both of those fucking cans between your toes."

Classic Hazing Tactic #5: If you happen to be dipping while talking to a pledge, purposely violate the "say it don't spray it" rule, firing tiny Stinger missiles of tobacco into said pledge's eyeballs.

In a display of double-dip hazing, The Maglite executed this move to perfection. My eyes stung from his spit as I frantically opened one can and then the other. What I was about to endure consists of filling the gaps between your toes with chewing tobacco and absorbing the nicotine through your feet, and it has many names: dip shoes, nicotine Nikes, snuff socks. All of them were being chanted by the other actives as they laughed and The Maglite hovered over me. He spiked his Miller Lite tallboy off the wall, missing my head by inches, and then crushed it beneath his boot.

"Well, boys," he yelled, "this fucking piece of shit ran into me on campus and didn't even know my *fucking* name!"

His voice echoed through the basement and the other actives started up the "ooooooooooh shit" chorus we had grown to fear.

"Look at my fucking face!" he screamed up and down the line. "Stop staring at the fucking ceiling and look at my face! My name is Jacob Delster, and the next time one of you doesn't know my name I'll make sure you never leave this fucking basement!"

I knelt down and he leaned over me and slapped me on the back of the head repeatedly, yelling, "Now mix every goddamn piece of dip from those cans in with your fucking toe jam!"

I took a giant, moist pinch between my fingers and thumb, squeezed it in between two toes, and then went on to the next gap. When I finished my right foot Mr. Stevens immediately wrapped it tightly with duct tape to make sure no dip fell out, and then forced my shoe back on. The intense smell of wintergreen that each can gave off made me nauseous as I moved to the left foot and repeated the process.

I slid on my left shoe and reassumed my position on the wall. The nicotine immediately rushed through my veins like a freight train. I was in a daze, and The Maglite could smell weakness.

"What's my name, motherfucker?"

My vision blurred, and I opened my mouth to speak, but all that came out was a line of drool. The Maglite leaned in toward me and screamed as loud as he could into my ear.

"I said...what, is, my, name, motherfucker!"

I couldn't feel my face. My mouth hung open with my tongue lazily resting against my bottom lip, like a bulldog on tranquilizers.

Then, in hazy slow motion, I watched The Maglite thrust his boulder-like head into mine with the power of a battering ram. I rocketed back into the wall and then collapsed to the floor. Mr. Weston and Mr. Harris restrained the violent legend as I felt my eyes flutter and pressed my hand to my forehead. When I pulled it back it was painted red.

There is an unwritten rule that creates a line not to be crossed when it comes to physical abuse of pledges, and it had just been crossed. Mr. Stevens stood over me with two fistfuls of his own hair, staring down at the bloody mess that was my face.

"Oh shit! Delster, you've got to get the fuck out of here."

He grabbed The Maglite by the arm and tried to pull him away as he kept shouting down at me.

"I said what's my fucking name, pledge! What's my fucking name!?"

Mr. Stevens pulled him harder, and as he stumbled toward the stairs The Maglite flung his half-finished beer inaccurately down the line to my left.

"Remember my fucking name!" he yelled. "Next time there won't be anyone to save you!"

In my foggy state I glanced up the staircase and saw him point right at me.

"I'm going to leave the imprint of my cock across your stupid fucking face!" Mr. Stevens slammed the door shut behind him, but I could still hear The Maglite shouting into the night.

I felt blood pouring from my nose as Rogers and Parsells took me by the arm and stood me up, holding me against the wall. Trendall took one look at my forehead, turned to Mr. Weston, and had a total fucking meltdown.

"Why are you doing this?" he cried out. "Look at his head!"

"Calm the fuck down, Trendall," said Mr. Weston. "Delster just had too much to drink, that's all."

"Are you kidding me? He could have killed him! Look at him! Look!"

Trendall started hyperventilating and dropped to the ground like a stone.

"God damn it, drag him outside and make sure he's okay," said Mr. Weston.

Monte picked Trendall up by his armpits and dragged him toward the stairs while Rogers and Parsells made sure I stayed awake. I heard Mr. Weston and Mr. Harris discussing what to do next.

"Just get them the fuck out of here!" hissed Mr. Harris.

"I'm going to, goddammit! Let me think!"

Mr. Weston walked over to me and wiped the blood from my forehead and nose with his shirtsleeve.

"Are you all right?" he asked.

"Yes sir," I responded.

"Good. Keep your fucking mouth shut."

He stepped back and addressed the line.

"Alpha business is Alpha business! If any of you tell anyone about what happened here tonight you will never come within a hundred feet of this house again! You don't tell your mommies; you don't tell your girlfriends; you don't tell your fucking priest. Got it?"

"Sir yes sir!" we rang out in unison.

"Say it! Alpha business is Alpha business!"

"SIR, ALPHA BUSINESS IS ALPHA BUSINESS, SIR!"

"Good. Now get the fuck out of here," he ordered.

That's when I learned the ironic fact that when hazing goes overboard—and it frequently does—it usually results in the end of the session. The actives don't want things to escalate any further. Any chance of a violent mob mentality taking over on their side, or ours, ends badly for everyone.

Parsells and Rogers supported me until we got outside and I started to regain my senses.

"I'm all right," I said as I shook them off and felt the gash on my head. "Do I need to go to the fucking emergency room?"

Tim walked over and wiped my cut with the pocket linen from his blazer.

"It's not deep," he said. "You'll be fine, but I guess that's what you get for fucking us."

Monte slapped me on the back. "Trendall came to, but I'm pretty sure he's having a panic attack and headed to the dorm for some meds. Think you've got a concussion?"

I shook my head no. As we filed toward the parking lot I remembered I still had two fresh cans of Grizzly contaminating my blood. I couldn't even feel my forehead, because the nicotine had numbed my senses completely. I sat down on the curb and took my shoes off, and then Tim and Monte helped pull the duct tape from my feet.

I threw up twice when I got back to my dorm, and pulled black dusty boogers from my nose the next morning. As stupid as it sounds, I felt a sense of accomplishment I had never known. I had survived.

———

Pledgeship differs from chapter to chapter across the country, but houses that uphold the sacred traditions passed down from generation to generation go through very similar shit storms. These shit storms are what bond the pledges together with a shared experience that they will tell stories about, laugh about, and cry about for the rest of their lives...

On Pledgeship and Hazing

Hazing is like a taint. It separates the pussies from the assholes. TFM.

Rudolph was the only reindeer that got hazed and look how well he turned out. TFM.

Signing the anti-hazing agreement on a pledge's back. TFM.

Pledgerism—the art of having a pledge write your paper. TFM.

Any sentence that starts with "pledge" is a command. TFM.

Explaining to the Greek Life coordinator that the pledges that were blindfolded and walking through campus were actually participating in a visually impaired diversity exercise. TFM.

Just like the rules, pledges were made to be broken. TFM.

We may have the worst pledge class in chapter history, but it's still the best one on campus. TFM.

EDITORS' NOTE: For obvious reasons, nobody takes pictures of hazing.

Hell Week

WE HAD LOST THREE PLEDGE BROTHERS ALONG THE way. One had a complete emotional breakdown during week six, withdrew from the university, and was never heard from again. Another's dad told him he could choose between quitting pledgeship and paying his own tuition after he dropped a class halfway through the semester. The third made the mistake of telling Mr. Weston he planned on transferring to another school his sophomore year. Mr. Weston chased him out of the house and told him if he ever saw him on campus he'd rip out his "fucking traitor spleen." The actives made us vow never to mention their names again.

For the thirty-nine of us who remained, after eleven long weeks of misery, the light at the end of the tunnel was finally visible. The idea of initiation should have served as motivation to finish strong, but the collective morale of our group had been completely shattered. Misery and exhaustion warped the faces that had arrived on campus just months before with bright eyes and excited smiles. We were bruised, scratched, scarred, and worn. Even Tim's personality had dulled from the erosion of mental torment. I tried to convince myself that the worst was over, but it wasn't, and nothing would compare to the living hell that awaited.

It was storming hard on the twelfth Monday night of our pledge semester, and rain pounded against our window as Monte and I sat awake on our beds, staring at the TV with dead eyes. Thunder shook the very foundation of Manor Hall, but neither of us flinched, too exhausted to give a shit if the building collapsed, but unable to sleep because we had been told to expect a call. It was past midnight and still no word.

My head bobbed as I nodded off for one sweet second before the phone rang and sent me scrambling to my feet. Mr. Weston's name popped up on the screen with a high-definition picture of his left nut that he'd forced me to use as his photo ID. I froze while it rang again and again until Monte reacted.

"Fucking answer it!" he yelled. I snapped out of it and grabbed the iPhone off my dresser.

"Sir, Alpha pledge Townes Prescott, how are you today, Mr. Weston, sir?"

"Wake the fuck up," he said. "Blue jeans, white T-shirt, and work boots. Pack your backpack with your pledge handbook, the books you need for class this week, and nothing else. Be lined up in the basement by 1 a.m., and bring a copy of your schedule."

"Sir yes sir," I said.

"Tell Montgomery too." *Click.*

I knew exactly what was going on. It was no secret. The actives had been strategically holding it over our heads since the beginning of pledgeship.

"You think this is hard? Wait until Hell Week, you fucking pussy."

Hell Week was the final stage of pledgeship. Unfortunately,

the definition of a "week" seemed to vary wildly throughout the history of Alpha. Some actives said it was five nights, others said seven. Atwater told me about one pledge class in the 1980s that fucked up so royally, their Hell Week lasted two full weeks.

I forced speculation to the back of my mind as I put on my jeans and boots, then stuffed my backpack with the books I needed for class.

"Am I allowed to bring contact solution?" asked Monte. "My toothbrush? Toothpaste?"

"I don't know. Mr. Weston said *nothing* else."

"Fuck Mr. Weston," he said. "I'm bringing it."

We zipped up our bags and I hit the lights on the way out of our room, oblivious to the fact that I'd soon be begging for the comfort of my shitty twin-sized dorm bed. On the way down the hall I noticed that Monte's jaw was clinched tight, and he had fear in his eyes like a fighter about to step into the ring against an undefeated opponent.

The thunderstorm raged on as I drove toward the house with my windshield wipers on high. I found myself praying for a wreck or some kind of traffic obstacle to slow our approach to inevitable pain, but nothing came. When I pulled into the parking lot I saw Mr. Harris sitting in a lawn chair under a giant umbrella, wearing a yellow poncho, holding a clipboard and flashlight. Mr. Harris was one of Mr. Weston's best friends, and as a result was always highly involved in hazing, like a top-ranking demon in Satan's army. He stood up and directed me into a tight spot between a Range Rover and an F-150.

"Give me your fucking keys," he yelled over the rain as I slammed my door shut.

I tossed them to him, and he dropped them into a plastic bag filled with dozens of others.

"You know where to go," he yelled, pointing up toward the house.

Monte and I ran through the downpour and joined most of our pledge class who were already waiting under the veranda as shelter from the shower. We were ordered never to enter the basement until every single one of us was present, and rain didn't change that rule.

Rogers and Trendall jogged up behind us while Parsells did a head count.

"Can't we just go in?" asked Trendall, wiping his face with his sleeve. "This is ridiculous!"

"No, Trendall, we can't, and you fucking know it," said Parsells.

A bolt of lightning lit up the sky.

"I'm going to get fucking electrocuted!" Trendall squeaked, ducking down behind Monte.

We ignored him and waited in silence.

A few minutes later all thirty-nine of us were there, and we headed down into the basement together.

There were candles burning in each corner, giving an eerie light to the normally dark underground room, and a large, solid wood table in the middle. The air was even thicker than usual thanks to the rain, and the old couch and other broken furniture that were usually scattered around the basement were piled at one end, like someone had tidied up the place to make room for more people. As we lined up in our positions there was no need to shout names. We knew where to go. We had done it so many times that getting in alphabetical order took less than ten seconds.

"Well, we made it this far, right?" joked Rogers as he filed in next to me.

Another blast of thunder killed the small talk, and then the door at the top of the stairs swung open into the wall like it had so many times before. Mr. Weston walked briskly down the steps with a clipboard and pen in hand. There was a sense of purpose and urgency in his stride. Mr. Harris, Mr. Stevens, and Mr. Brewster followed closely behind him.

"Take off your fucking backpacks and put them at your feet," shouted Mr. Weston as he stopped at the table, never looking up from his clipboard.

We all swung our bags around and dropped them to our feet as the actives spread out among us. Mr. Brewster immediately grabbed my bag, unzipped it, and turned it upright, spilling my books on the floor.

"Did you pack me anything special?" he asked. He kicked my books around and looked up at me with disappointment.

"You bore the shit out of me, you know that, Prescott?"

He moved on to Parsells's backpack. Mr. Harris and Mr. Stevens were busy checking others.

The mixture of sweat and rainwater dripping from my hair stung my eyes as their search continued, and another blast of thunder shook the room as Mr. Stevens tore into Monte.

"Mr. Weston said to bring your books and class schedule. He didn't say anything about your fucking toothbrush, toothpaste, or your fucking stoner eyedrops!"

I could tell he wasn't joking. Mr. Stevens genuinely assumed Monte's contact solution was drops used to cure the redness that comes with smoking weed.

"Do you need your wittle eyedroppies to stop the burning in your bloodshot hippie eyes?" he asked condescendingly.

Mr. Stevens unscrewed the cap and splashed the bottle out onto Monte's crotch, then picked the toothpaste off the ground and squeezed the entire tube onto the top of Monte's head before moving on to the next person's backpack. Other actives were heading down the stairs to get a piece of the action.

"I know at least one of you dumbasses packed something interesting!" yelled Mr. Harris.

Just then, Mr. Brewster found something.

"Are you fucking kidding me, Trendall?"

Suddenly all the actives in the room were focused on Trendall, laughing with amusement. Even Mr. Weston let out a chuckle.

"Jesus Christ, that's the biggest bag of Skittles I've ever seen," said Mr. Stevens.

"Look…look at the size of this fucking bag!" said Mr. Brewster, fighting to stifle his laughter. "You jackasses can stop looking at the ceiling. Look at this!"

I looked over at the two-gallon Ziploc bag, packed to the brim with Skittles.

"Were you planning on eating fucking Skittles until you got diabetes, then using that as an excuse to go to the health center?" asked Mr. Harris.

Laughter filled the room again.

"You think that's funny?" Mr. Weston boomed over the others.

He stomped over, snatched the bag from Mr. Harris's hand, opened it, and stared directly into Trendall's eyes while he took a handful of candy.

"Everyone thinks your snack is funny, Trendall," Mr. Weston said. "Let's see if you find this amusing."

He picked up one leg like a pitcher on the mound and

flung Skittles into Trendall's face as hard as he could. Trendall recoiled and dropped to the floor, shielding himself while Mr. Harris took another handful and peppered him in the back.

"Is this fucking funny?" Mr. Weston shouted as he took another handful. "Is everyone getting a good fucking laugh?"

He wildly flung another handful down the line in my direction. One Skittle struck me in the cheek. I was fifteen feet away and it still stung.

Mr. Weston dropped to one knee and pulled Trendall's head back by the hair.

"Open your mouth! Open it and look at me!"

Trendall let out a pathetic whine as he opened his mouth and Mr. Weston slapped in a fistful of Skittles.

"Is this satisfying your fucking sweet tooth?" Mr. Weston yelled in his face while he covered Trendall's mouth with his hand.

Trendall coughed and tried to chew, and then Mr. Weston pushed his head into the dirt while the rest of us looked on in horror.

"God damn it!" Mr. Weston yelled, standing to his feet. "You don't give a shit if we initiate you, do you?"

He dumped the hundreds of remaining Skittles from the giant bag into the dirt.

"You want to prove that you care about this fraternity?" he asked loudly.

"Sir yes sir!" we answered.

"You have one minute to have every single one of those fucking candies in your stomachs," he said. "Now!"

Imagine thirty-nine starving rats fighting over crumbs of cheese. That's exactly what we looked like for the next forty-five seconds. Guys were scooping handfuls of Skittles and dirt into their mouths like it was water from the fountain of youth. At one point I was down on both knees pushing Monte's foot out of the way so I could grab for a Skittle he had accidentally covered with his shoe. The actives rained insults down on us as we finished them all, and then we scrambled back to our spots, faces and teeth freckled with dirt, fingers sticky with sugar.

"Welcome to Hell Week, boys!" Mr. Weston yelled, smiling menacingly.

The actives filled the room with sarcastic claps and cheers that made my stomach churn with anxiety.

"I hope you worms enjoyed that, because it was the last fucking meal you're ever going to have," someone toward the back yelled.

Mr. Weston raised his hands to silence the growing crowd.

"During this week our house is your home," he said. "The only time you leave this house is to go to class, and when class ends you'll sprint back here immediately. Stack your class schedules and your cell phones on this table one by one in order. If you're not back within ten minutes of class there will be hell to pay. If anyone asks why you look like shit, why you smell like shit, or any other questions, you tell them it is *house appreciation week* and you're working on a major project. Do we understand each other?"

"Sir yes sir!" we responded.

"You will not sleep. You will not eat. If you're caught doing either I will make you wish you never escaped from your mother's snatch. To start house appreciation week you're going to clean the fucking house until it tastes like lemons, smells like daisies, and looks brand-fucking-new."

He took a piece of paper from his clipboard with ASSIGN-

MENTS scribbled on the top and stuck it to the wall with a thumbtack.

For the rest of the night we cleaned nonstop without a wink of sleep. I swept, mopped, and dusted like a fucking houseboy for seven straight hours. Other guys painted, made repairs to the house, did the actives' laundry, and cleaned their rooms. They were hounding us in shifts, and I never went more than a few minutes without being verbally harassed.

"You mop like shit, Prescott. Put your fucking back into it! How can I trust you as a brother if you can't even properly mop my fucking floor?"

We were spread out all over the house, but so were they. When one guy got tired of yelling, another replaced him. As the hours passed my mind kicked into autopilot and I lost track of time completely. We weren't allowed to wear watches, our phones had been taken, and all the clocks in the house had been changed to wildly disagree.

After I finished mopping the dining room I headed to the kitchen to refill my bucket and heard Turbo talking to Mr. Stevens while he swept.

"Sir, I have class at eight o'clock. Do you mind if I ask what time it is, sir?"

"It's time for you to eat everything in that dustpan," said Mr. Stevens.

I stopped and watched as Turbo picked up the dustpan, slowly tilted his head back, and opened his mouth as if he were waiting for Mr. Stevens to tell him he was kidding. Then he poured the dirt, sand, and dust into his pie hole, coughing it back up all over himself.

"We'll tell you what time it is when you need to fucking know," said Mr. Stevens.

They had completely brainwashed us. We were totally under their control.

As the sun came up I was raking the volleyball pit for the third time when Mr. Weston came outside in his white bathrobe, holding a cup of coffee.

"Good morning, boys!" he said, condescending sarcasm dripping from his every word. "Don't you love waking up to a clean house after a great night's sleep? It's seven o'clock, time to gather up in the dining room for a little powwow."

Once we were all inside he told us that he would be broadcasting the time every hour on the fifty-minute mark with a megaphone to make sure we attended class. I had history at 9 a.m. and spent the rest of the morning passing time with mundane task after mundane task, waiting for the 8:50 announcement.

When it finally came I ran down to the basement, grabbed my backpack, and headed out into the real world. Other students eyed me curiously as I walked through the quad in my grimy off-white shirt and filthy jeans. We were on the same campus, but we were in two totally different worlds, and they had no fucking idea.

Before entering the lecture hall I stopped in the bathroom, washed my hands, splashed water on my face, and dried myself off with a paper towel. In the mirror I could see tired bags of stress forming under my eyes. I had only survived one night of Hell Week and already looked like a bum who'd been sleeping under a bridge for months.

During my first class I let the sweet serenity that came with being out of the Alpha house wash over me, but I didn't hear a single word my professor said. After history I headed to my ten o'clock English class, sat in the back row, and passed out immediately. I woke up when the kid next to me stood to leave, wiped the drool from my face, and shuffled out.

I power-walked back through the quad. There was no way I was going to be the one to find out the punishment for taking more than ten minutes to return to the house. When I jogged up I saw two guys using push mowers on the lawn, two others wielding weed eaters, and several others reinforcing the balcony with hammers and nails. Some of the guys who didn't have morning classes had been working since 1:30 a.m. the night before. None of them so much as lifted an eye to acknowledge my arrival.

I headed down to the basement, put my backpack in my spot, and checked the posted paper to see what my assignment for the day was. I was to paint the entire second-floor hallway a new coat of white.

That took around six hours, but I worked relatively undisturbed except for the passing jests of actives headed to and from class. Later that evening Mr. Stevens gathered the entire pledge class in the dining room and began testing us on the pledge handbook. It wasn't so bad, and I caught myself thinking that maybe tonight would be easy. But night came too soon, and with it, Mr. Weston.

He stumbled into the dining room with a dip in his bottom lip and a bottle of Jim Beam in his hand, staggered into the wall, knocking off an old paddle, and spit out a string of curses.

"God damn it bullshit fucking pledges!"

He picked up the paddle, squinted and swayed while he extended his arm, pointing the wooden weapon at the thirty-nine of us sitting cross-legged on the dining room floor.

"Basement!" he yelled. "BASEMENT!"

I had never seen him so enraged, or so obviously shitfaced. Mr. Stevens shut the pledge handbook as we scrambled to our feet and sprinted out down the hall.

We were lined up in the dark for five minutes before Mr. Weston finally rammed through the basement door and slammed it shut behind him. I could barely make out his shadowy figure against the light coming through the crack at the bottom of the doorway as he walked slowly down the stairs, either taking his time to torture us or making sure he didn't fall. I lost sight of him when he blended in with the darkness, but I could hear his heavy, angry breathing as he paced back and forth in front of us without a word. For several minutes we stood in silence, wondering what we'd done, what our punishment would be, and what was coming next.

"One of you was spotted leaving your dorm today," he finally muttered.

The basement door opened again and three other actives entered carrying what looked like huge bags. Mr. Weston let out a huge belch and went on talking like he knew they were coming.

"You're an embarrassment to this fraternity, and you're a fucking stain on my reputation as pledgemaster. I'm going to watch you do bows and toes on fucking lava rocks until one of you fesses up. If you confess, then the rest of your pledge brothers will stop suffering. We'll sit here all fucking night if we have to!"

Mr. Weston flicked on the lights and the safety of darkness could no longer hide the fear in our eyes. Mr. Harris, Mr. Stevens, and Mr. Brewster were walking up and down the line dumping lava rocks at our feet.

"Does anyone want to confess?" asked Mr. Weston. Nobody said a word.

"Then get the fuck down!"

I dropped to the ground and tried to grind my arms through the layers of lava rocks to find the comfort of dirt, but there were too many. I felt the calluses on my elbows tear immediately. Mr. Weston guzzled down more whiskey from his handle as he stomped to the front of the line with the paddle at his side.

"You're supposed to go straight to class and come straight back!" he yelled. "You're just not getting it! I'm going to have to make you understand. Adams, do you confess?"

Adams, the first in our pledge class alphabetically, didn't have an answer.

"I said do you fucking confess!" said Mr. Weston. "No? Then stand the fuck up, pull down your jeans, bend over, and grab your nuts."

"Be sure and pull those little raisins forward," said Mr. Harris.

I looked up from the floor to see Adams bent over at the waist with his hands gripping his balls as Mr. Weston reared back with the paddle and then swung it forward with the weight of his entire body behind it. The crack of wood against bare ass flesh sent chills up my already aching spine. Adams jolted forward but managed to stay on his feet.

"Get the fuck back down on your elbows!" Mr. Weston yelled. "Who's next?"

One by one he asked for a confession and delivered a powerful stroke of thick wooden justice to the backside of each member of my pledge class.

It felt like we were on bows and toes for an eternity, and my legs started violently shaking with fatigue. Twice I had to quickly drop my knees to the ground for a momentary breather. By the time it was my turn to face the paddle I decided there was no reason to wait for Mr. Weston's question, stood to my feet, and felt blood drip down my left forearm as I pulled down my jeans to expose my cheeks.

"Looks like someone has a guilty conscience," said Mr. Weston. "It was you, wasn't it, Prescott?"

"Sir no sir," I responded firmly as I pulled my nuts forward to keep them from getting clipped.

I closed my eyes as he loaded back in his stance.

"You think you can sleep in your dorm while the rest of your pledge brothers suffer?" he asked.

"Sir no sir!"

The power of the wood colliding with my ass sent a shockwave of pain through my hamstrings and lower back. I grunted in agony, but held in my screams like my pledge brothers before me.

"Was it you, Prescott?" Mr. Stevens yelled in my face.

"Sir no sir!"

Mr. Weston swung again and the paddle landed flush against my left cheek. It went numb as I stumbled forward.

"My arms are getting tired!" he yelled. "Will you take one more paddle to save the asses of the eight pieces of shit in line behind you?"

"Sir yes sir!" I said without hesitation.

"Then assume the fucking position!"

For the grand finale he stepped back three feet and crow-hopped into his swing to make sure he got his money's worth. I couldn't hold in my pain and yelped like an injured dog on impact as the strength of the blow broke the paddle in half on my ass, along with my skin. I immediately lost feeling in both of my legs from the knees up. The top half of the fragmented paddle hit the ground behind me as excruciating pain shot up through my backbone and sent me toppling over face first into the dirt.

"WOOOOH!" Mr. Weston howled. "That's what I'm fucking talking about!"

He stood above me like a hunter over his kill as I held my hands behind my back, covering my battered cheeks.

"Everybody on your feet! Pledge Prescott's ass just earned you thirty minutes to figure out which one of you is the traitor while I go find another paddle. When I come back I want some fucking answers."

I refused to uncover my ass as Rogers and Parsells pulled me to my knees and Mr. Weston stomped up the stairs with his handle of liquor turned upright. The others followed him, and when they shut the door I pulled my jeans back up slowly.

Mr. Weston returned thirty minutes later with a paddle twice as thick as the one he'd broken over my backside, and he only had to ask once.

"Who the fuck went to their dorm?"

All thirty-nine of us answered as one.

"SIR, I DID, SIR!"

He smiled, set the paddle down on the table, turned, and started back up the stairs, stopping on the top step to turn around and address us.

"You pieces of shit are finally starting to see how things work around here," he said. "I might even let you get some sleep tonight."

That last part was a lie. We were left alone for no more than ten minutes before the first group of three actives came in and lined us up. They drank the entire time as they quizzed us on the lives of actives in the fraternity, made us recite the Greek alphabet, and punished the entire pledge class every time someone got an answer wrong. We did bows and toes, wall sits, bear crawls, push-ups, tuned the TV, and endured an endless verbal assault. They left when they'd had their fill, and just when we got comfortable being alone again another group of three came through the door and the madness started all over again. That vicious cycle continued all night, and we were still being hazed when Mr. Weston came in and announced that it was 7:50 a.m.

On Day 3 almost everyone was "going to class," but actually going back to their dorms, power napping and eating in solitude. We had learned that no matter what we did the hazing would continue, so why not get some fucking food in our stomachs and a few winks of sleep? We couldn't shower, of course; that would be too obvious.

That afternoon I borrowed Monte's key and got a flawless hour and a half of shuteye during my two-hour block of classes. I dreamt that I was back at home, swimming in my parents' pool without a worry in the world, but when my alarm went off the rest of Hell Week was still waiting for me. I took the back exit from Manor to make sure I wasn't seen leaving.

After a few more hours of bitch work, on our third night we were separated into four groups. We learned more about the founding fathers, memorized sacred passages, and took turns reciting parts of the pledge handbook. We were tested repeatedly, and anytime one of us forgot an answer we were punished while a team of actives screamed in our faces until we remembered correctly, as usual.

That was the easy part.

Around 2 a.m. Mr. Weston lined us up in the main hallway of the first floor.

"You are beginning a three-night test of character that will show if you have the qualities required to be my brother," he said. "Tonight you will experience the Alpha Funhouse. Get down to the fucking basement!"

We ran toward the basement in unison, maintaining our alphabetical order like a well-trained military platoon. It was a cloudy night, so very little moonlight made its way inside our dungeon, and I bounced off a few guys before making my way between Parsells and Rogers up against the back wall. Then the door at the top of the stairs slammed shut and I could barely make out my hand as I held it out in front of me.

"Fuck," I heard Trendall whisper. His anxiety had worsened with his lack of sleep.

I stared into the abyss as my eyes adjusted, listening to the panting of my pledge brothers and waiting for the actives to come screaming into the room, when suddenly I felt something crawling up my leg. I reached down and slapped it off. Then I heard Rogers gasp.

"What the fuck was that?" he whispered.

My brain caught up with my ears and I realized the room was chirping. The fucking basement was crawling with crickets.

The sound system turned on and "Hip to Be Square" blared through the speakers. I brushed another cricket off my shoulder and cupped my hand over Rogers's ear.

"This fucking song is going to play all night!"

"No shit!" he yelled back.

It was psychological warfare. The song restarted five times before I finally began to snap. When the beat kicked back on for the sixth time I felt my right eye twitching with tension. Every few seconds another cricket jumped onto me, and eventually I stopped caring enough to shake them off. They must have bought thousands from a pet store and released them while we were learning upstairs. I started stomping aimlessly at the ground below me, hoping that I'd kill some in the process.

After an hour or so I felt Parsells slump back into the wall and sink to the ground. I leaned over to him.

"What the fuck are you doing? Mr. Weston could come down here any second."

"He's not coming," he yelled back. "I'm not standing up all fucking night for nothing."

He was probably right, and if one of us was sitting we might as well all sit. I went to the front of the line and one by one told the guys it was okay to take a breather. Some protested, but they caved when they saw the guys to their left and right sitting down.

After a while madness began to take hold, and Rogers and Parsells sang along with Huey Lewis and the News on either side of me. I joined in and heard someone to my left scream out in annoyance, his voice barely carrying over the blasting music. The song played exactly fifteen times an hour for five straight hours while crickets crawled all over us. Seventy-five straight plays. It was pure hell.

When morning came and the music finally shut off, I heard Mr. Weston's megaphone booming through the door.

"It's 7:50, kids, time to get to your eight o'clock classes. The rest of you, get back to work."

Throughout the entire day, both in class and while I worked back at the house, "Hip to Be Square" was stuck in my head.

When Night 4 came I could tell something was different. Mr. Brewster even asked me how I was holding up.

"Sir?" I responded.

"I said, how you are feeling?"

I just nodded, because my brain was unable to compute what was happening. He shook his head, looked at me like I was crazy, and walked away.

That night we were locked in the entertainment room and forced to watch *The Shining* at maximum volume while smells from the actives working in the kitchen next door seeped through the walls. We knew exactly what was coming, but none of us dared to bring it up.

Eventually Mr. Harris came in shouting.

"Let's go, motherfuckers! All work and no play makes Jack a fucking pledge! Down to the basement! Go! Go! Go! Go!"

We jogged out, and on my way past the kitchen the foul smell of their cooking raped my nostrils. We headed downstairs and I saw that another large wooden table had been set up with two thirty-two-gallon trash cans on either side of it. Mr. Weston was standing between the two tables in a chef's hat and a red apron that had KISS THE COOK printed across the chest in red letters.

"Gentlemen!" he said. "Your reservation for thirty-nine at the Alpha Cafeteria is ready."

Panic didn't set in. My stomach didn't even churn. The receptors in my brain were too tired to communicate emotion. The fight-or-flight reaction had been shut off. I simply filed into my spot, stared up at the ceiling, and awaited my fate.

Actives filed into the room until it was packed, and some spectators were forced to position themselves on the staircase. Mr. Stevens and Mr. Brewster entered wearing medical masks and carrying a giant cauldron that was still giving off steam. They placed it down onto one of the tables as Mr. Atwater and

Mr. Harris followed behind them with another huge pot, also wearing masks that covered their mouths and noses.

"I have twenty trays here," Mr. Weston said as he handed them out. "Two of you per tray, and Rumsen will have his own tray because he looks hungry."

Parsells and I were paired up, and we glanced at each other as we each grabbed one end of what would serve as our plate for the night.

"We have prepared a lovely five-course meal for you, and you're going to eat every fucking bite of it."

The actives laughed and clapped together, sipping beers, cracking jokes, and smoking cigarettes as they looked on. Mr. Weston rang a dinner bell to quiet the room and get everyone's attention.

"For your appetizer I've prepared a rare delicatessen," he said.

He picked up a large Tupperware container from under one of the tables, walked down the line, and placed two small round mystery treats on each tray. I stared down at the white ball that appeared to be sprinkled with some kind of seasoning.

"Dig in," said Mr. Weston. The roar of the actives filled the room with the stench of terrible inevitability.

I figured I might as well get it over with, so I grabbed the ball and put it in my mouth whole. It was much harder than I expected, with a horribly spicy taste. I crunched my teeth down through it and chewed as fast as I could, praying that my taste buds would malfunction as every muscle in my face tightened.

"Swallow those balls!" someone yelled. "Let them slide deep down into your throat."

"What you're enjoying is a ball of ginger sprinkled with

Copenhagen snuff," said Mr. Weston. "I hope you like it, because that's the best fucking thing you're going to taste all night."

It was fucking disgusting. Rogers gagged next to me as I forced myself to swallow the last remaining bit.

"Look at this!" said Mr. Weston, carrying a gallon milk jug filled with brown liquid. "I was kind enough to make you all a smoothie to wash it down. It had better be completely fucking empty by the time it gets to Washington."

Adams took his swig and started coughing as he passed the jug. A few seconds later I heard the first splatter of throw-up hit the dirt.

"Don't you dare throw up on my beautiful basement floor!" said Mr. Stevens. "You throw up in the goddamn trash cans. That's why we brought them down here, you fucking retard."

Adams stumbled toward the closest trash can, supported himself with his hands on either side, and spewed a brown river through the air into the bin. The room filled with the same resounding "ohhhhh" that you hear during the goriest scene in a horror film.

By the time the jug got to me it was a little under half-way empty, and there were only eight guys to go. I was going to have to take a huge hit. Adams was the only one who had barfed, and I figured he had just mentally psyched himself out, so I held my nose and took a gulp.

"Chug that shit down, Prescott!" yelled Mr. Harris.

It was the worst taste I had ever experienced in my life, and I caught a burp in my mouth to keep from vomiting. The actives rooted me on.

"Don't fuck your pledge brothers!"

I took another deep breath, pressed the plastic to my lips,

and opened my throat. After I'd taken as much as I could I quickly passed the jug on to Rogers and put both hands on the top of my head, taking slow breaths to calm my gag reflex. Luckily, when the jug reached Washington at the end of the line he only had to take a few sips to polish it off.

"I hope you enjoyed that refreshment," said Mr. Weston. "That was two days' worth of my dip spit mixed with milk, some pubes, and one clump of my dog's shit."

Trendall lunged toward the trash can and puked while several actives huddled around him and informed him that he had the stomach of a prepubescent girl.

"It's time for the second course," announced Mr. Weston. He grabbed two brown grocery bags from under the other table and started passing out sandwiches.

It looked totally normal from the outside, and there was no fucking way I was going to open it for an examination, so I took a huge bite out of the middle and immediately spit it back onto our tray.

"You eat that shit off of your tray, Prescott!" yelled Mr. Brewster. "Every single fucking bite! If you spit it out, you eat it back up!"

The sandwich was packed with cigarettes and sprinkled with some kind of incredibly slimy pepper dressing. Dry tobacco sucked the moisture from my mouth, and chewing was damn-near impossible. I begged my body to create more saliva as I tried to swallow another bite.

"That's an entire pack of Marlboros between two delicious slices of wheat bread, accompanied by a light sauce made up of green jalapeño Tabasco and vinegar," said Mr. Weston.

I fought to get another bite down, and it slowly scraped its way through my throat to my grumbling stomach. Rogers nudged me in the arm as he stumbled forward and threw up all over his own boots before he could reach the trash can.

"In the fucking trash can!" Mr. Stevens yelled, pushing Rogers in the back.

Rogers stumbled closer, but the next blast came flying out of his gullet too soon, and he painted the side of the trash can with yack. That caused a chain reaction. Monte rushed over to the other trash can and launched his insides into it, and Trendall followed behind him, holding his stomach as he ran. The actives cheered victoriously every time another one of our stomachs rejected the Hell Week cuisine.

Parsells was dry-heaving between every bite as we battled to finish off the cig sandwiches, but Mr. Weston was ready to move on.

"It's time for the main course!"

He motioned to Mr. Harris and Mr. Brewster, and they picked up the giant cauldron while Mr. Weston wielded a ladle.

"Who's ready for some enchiladas?" Mr. Weston yelled as he started serving. "Eat it with your fucking hands. You don't deserve spoons."

The cauldron wasn't even halfway to me when Adams headed to the trash can again. Christopher, who was third in line, couldn't hold it down either and followed behind, unloading the contents of his stomach all over Adams's back. I watched as Adams's face turned green.

"Get your fucking ass inside that trash can, Adams!" Mr. Weston yelled, pointing at Adams with his ladle. "If you can't keep my food down you'll join it in that fucking can!"

Adams threw one leg over the side and stepped into the sea of puke.

"Crouch down, you ungrateful little shit," Mr. Weston commanded. Then he turned back to the line and finally reached my tray.

The slop he served looked like watered-down lasagna that had been rotting for weeks, and smelled like sewage. It wasn't even close to resembling enchiladas, but I decided to man up and bury my face in the tray.

As I slurped away at the liquid sludge I heard Parsells dry-heave and picked up my head just in time to watch him throw up directly onto our tray, mixing his bile in with our alleged Mexican dinner. My psyche took a big hit. The actives' cheers suddenly seemed far away and muffled, and the room spun around me as Parsells used his hand to scoop his own vomit from the tray back to his mouth.

"Holy fucking shit!" said Mr. Brewster.

I heard Mr. Weston's voice egging Parsells on. "That's right! You're a fucking animal!"

Parsells snapped. The crazy-eyed look of a man filled with the determination and drive to survive took hold of him as he shoveled everything from our tray into his mouth. My food, his food, his puke...he swallowed all of it. I stood in awe as he reached over to Monte's tray, grabbed a handful of his food, and downed it as well.

The sight of his collapse was as much as I could take, so I tapped him on the back to let him know I was evacuating. Then I let go of my end of the tray and sprinted toward the trash can at the far end of the room, as the other one was already surrounded. Turbo reached it at the same time as me, and we collided as I sent my projectile mouth diarrhea sailing into Adams's hair as he covered his face with his hands. As I leaned over with drool streaming from my mouth and tried to apologize I felt someone stagger up behind me. Whoever it was hurled all over my back and neck, causing my own gag reflex to trigger once again.

"What you're eating is old oatmeal mixed with melted cheese, jalapeños, and around twenty bottles of Tabasco," Mr. Weston announced as I fought through the crowd that surrounded the trash can. "It was marinated in the kitchen sink with used Band-Aids and condoms, and topped off with a long stream of piss from Mr. Harris."

My mind went numb and throw-up dripped down the crack of my ass as I squeezed back into my spot on the line and grabbed one side of the tray. I glanced over at Parsells, who was breathing heavily, with slop hanging from his lips and chin.

"The enchiladas weren't so bad," he said.

"Yeah." That was the only response I could muster. We had both gone into shock.

By the time the next course came around I felt like someone had poured battery acid down my throat. I was sweating profusely, and could feel my head pounding from dehydration.

"I think you guys need a palate cleanser," said Mr. Weston.

The actives roared in response.

We were each served a sardine, completely covered in wasabi. I took it down in one gulp without even flinching, and couldn't taste the sardine because the wasabi was too strong to give way to any other flavors. My body was in survival mode, running on nothing but adrenaline. I stood with my left hand over my mouth and my right hand holding up our tray, waiting for whatever came next.

"Who wants an ice cream cone for dessert?" asked Mr. Weston.

He wasn't lying about the cones, but instead of ice cream

there was a giant blob of Crisco stuff with dog food and sprinkled with dip. I attacked it aggressively like a starving child who had just been handed a turkey leg. After I finished it off I looked at Parsells, who had only managed to eat half of his and was just standing there staring at the rest of it. He couldn't take it anymore. I grabbed the cone from his hand and crushed it into my face. Around half of it ended up on the floor, but nobody seemed to notice.

Suddenly applause filled the room, and for once the booming cheers of the actives seemed completely congratulatory instead of sarcastic and demeaning. I looked down the line and saw some of my pledge brothers smiling with a sense of accomplishment. Others bent over and spit into the dirt, or held their hands over their mouths.

"Well done, boys!" Mr. Weston yelled. "Well done! You've survived Alpha Cafeteria. I swear on this house that the rest of the night is yours to actually get some fucking sleep."

Several actives walked down the stairs carrying crates of water and set them down on the two wooden tables. Atwater followed with a plastic bag filled with bottles of Pepto-Bismol.

"Get yourselves rehydrated," said Mr. Weston. "You'll find every cap is sealed, so don't worry—the water hasn't been fucked with. Oh, and if you haven't already, I recommend making yourself throw everything up before drinking that Pepto. Otherwise you'll take the most painful shit of your life."

Then he and the other actives filed up the stairs and shut the door behind them.

I had survived the most traumatizing night of my life, and even though I was pretty sure I was going to die from a stomach ulcer, I had finally earned some sleep. Granted, that sleep came on the floor of a basement covered in puke that smelled like a Dumpster, but it was sleep nonetheless.

I woke to the sound of Mr. Weston's 7:50 a.m. megaphone announcement, and walked over to check the freshly posted assignment sheet with the rest of the guys. It read FIGURE IT OUT, so we all headed upstairs to find a chore. I grabbed a broom from the pledge closet and pushed it around the house aimlessly. Every pledge brother I passed was just going through the motions as well. Turbo was dragging a mop behind him as he walked in circles around the kitchen. Rogers was adding coat after coat of paint to the same spot on the living room wall, completely zoned out. I actually watched Nate hammer the same nail into the porch railing for five whole minutes while I swept.

The actives completely ignored us the entire morning, and when I got back from class not a single one of them could be seen.

"Where the fuck is everyone?" I asked Monte.

"I got back at nine o'clock and haven't seen a single active since," he said. "Neither has anyone else."

Through the entire afternoon we were the only ones in the house. Then at six o'clock, when all thirty-nine of us were back from class, Atwater walked in the front door wearing a suit and tie and carrying a duffel bag. He walked right past me without even blinking and said, "Grab everyone and line up in the dining room."

Atwater stood with a solemn expression on his face without saying a word as we got in order, checking his watch twice before he finally spoke.

"I'm going to cover each of your eyes individually," he said. "You're not to say a fucking word the rest of the time we're here, or on the way to our destination. You fucking idiots must've really done something to piss Mr. Weston off, because he's talking crazy that he's going to blackball every single one of you and take a huge spring pledge class to make up for it. I'm taking you to a meeting with President Harvey to decide what the fuck to do."

I knew immediately that he was completely full of shit. Atwater was always the nice guy, and they would never send him to take care of something like this. One by one he blindfolded us and led us onto what sounded and felt like a bus. Death metal blared the entire time as sharp turns and bumpy roads sent me bouncing up and down in my seat. When we finally came to a screeching halt at our destination someone grabbed me by the arm and led me off. When my feet hit the ground I heard Atwater's voice in my ear.

"Congratulations, motherfucker. You made it to initiation."

I can't go into any real detail, because we swore on pain of death never to reveal any of Alpha's ritual to outsiders, but it was the most surreal experience of my life. The nearly 150-year-old initiation ceremony was spooky, weird, and more moving than any religious service I'd ever attended. Several guys (not me) cried tears of joy from a combination of the emotion, stress, lack of sleep, and deprivation of healthy food. It went on for six hours, and when it was all over all 110 actives gave me the secret Alpha handshake and hugged me as their equal.

As I made my way back toward the bus, which was now filled with cases of beer, Mr. Weston approached and put one hand on my shoulder.

"From now on you call me Arthur," he said, extending his other hand. "Congratulations, Townes, you fucking made it."

"Yes sir, Mr.—I mean, Arthur."

I would never get used to that.

The shackles had been removed and I was on top of the fucking world. Every single horrific thing I'd been forced to do, say, and eat was completely worth it. I was a part of something much bigger than myself, and had a whole new world of opportunity in front of me, filled with sorority girls and a never-ending supply of alcohol.

———

Fraternities across the country utilize Hell Week as one final test before initiation. In order for the pledges to reach the finish line they must first endure the mentally and physically exhausting traditions that have been formed within the fraternity through generations of hazing. During a semester that is filled with humbling tasks, suffering, and abuse, Hell Week stands alone, but initiation is always waiting at the end of the tunnel...

On Hell Week

Betting cigarettes on which pledge will cry first during hell week. TFM.

Eating prime rib in front of the pledges during hell week. TFM.

The pledges' assignment for the week was to break a world record. TFM.

I thought I missed my 1:00 p.m. class, but I saw a pledge in the common room with both hands directly above his head and realized it was only noon. TFM.

Bending the truth at the hospital during hell week. TFM.

The pledges think they see light at the end of the tunnel. It's the hell week train. TFM.

Played porno on the bigscreen TV in the fratcastle and muted it. Had 2 pledges make the sounds. Funniest 30 minutes of my life. TFM.

Various smells randomly cause hell week flashbacks. TFM.

GDI referred to finals week as "hell week." If he only knew... TFM.

EDITORS' NOTE: For even more obvious reasons, nobody takes pictures of hell week.

Taking a nap during Hell Week. TFM.

Christmas Tree Pledge. TFM.

Tagging the pledges with emasculating balloons. TFM.

The Frat Castle

CHRISTMAS BREAK CAME AND WENT, AND I SPENT MY second semester trying to make up the ground I'd lost with my 1.75 pledge GPA. It was all worth it, though, because when I pulled a 3.25 my parents approved my move into the Alpha house, otherwise known as the frat castle, for sophomore year.

You know how monks dedicate themselves to a life of silence, or priests pledge themselves to a life of celibacy? Moving into the frat castle is like pledging yourself to a life of being twice as loud and fucking twice as much in order to make up for all the monks and priests in the world. It is an honor reserved for those who have shown they have the ability to maintain enrollment while upholding a reputation for constant inebriation.

The house is a little over $1.5 million of redbrick beauty, standing three stories tall and nine windows wide with four massive white Greek columns out front. Each bedroom sleeps one brother and is connected with a neighboring bedroom through a joint bathroom. During parties these bathrooms serve as meeting points for casual drug use, sexual strategizing, and other private pursuits. There are ten bedrooms in the main hallway of the first floor along with the dining room, living room, and kitchen.

The other fifteen bedrooms are spread throughout the hallways of the second floor, and the third floor is just storage with access to our notorious crow's nest that overlooks campus. The house sits almost directly in the middle of Greek Row, with the Delta and Sigma houses on either side.

The grounds outside the house are what really make it the total package. In the backyard, behind our party patio, is a full-length asphalt basketball court (donated by my dad, known as "the Prescott Pavement") and sand volleyball pit. Landscapers, who are paid for with part of our annual dues, come twice a month during the pledge offseason to keep up the hedges, cut the grass, rake the sand, and water the flowerbeds. A couple times a year they end up having to replace everything entirely because of plant alcohol poisoning, thousands of cigarette butts, rivers of piss, and spontaneous party fires.

With every hour that I called the house home I became more and more seduced by its energy of anarchy. The phrase "peer pressure" doesn't do justice to the subconscious mindset that forms within every resident moments after setting foot on the property. An ambulance, fire truck, and university police cruiser all visited the house on my first day for completely unrelated reasons. I've never felt more alive and so close to death at the same time.

On move-in day, I was in the middle of unpacking when Tim showed up wearing a tank top that said BACK TO BACK WORLD WAR CHAMPS with an American flag in the middle. Nobody called him by his real name anymore, because on Spring Break in Cancún he took four hits of ecstasy, snorted two grams of coke, and smoked an eighth of weed in a twenty-four-hour period. That's when he was dubbed "Turbo," and the name stuck permanently. During his infamous bender, when I told him we needed to leave the club at 5 a.m. to catch our flight home, he yelled, "I'm staying, man!" and continued grinding on random ass. We had no choice but to leave him in Mexico. He showed up at the frat house forty-eight hours later with no recollection of the night, asking why we left him.

Turbo claimed the bedroom next to mine, set a case of Natty down in the middle of our adjoining bathroom, and tossed one to me.

"Good summer break, bud?" I asked.

"Fucking amazing," he said, slamming a box down on his bed. "Railed two of my high school girlfriends and got a new driver."

He didn't really unpack, just tossed boxes around his room and rapped along to his iPod dock, polishing off beer after beer. I went out to my truck to grab my bedding, and when I came back in Turbo was sitting at my desk fucking with my computer.

"You got any tit pics on here?" he asked between sips.

"Not where you can find them."

"Whatever, man, it's Top Gun time. Quit making your bed like a fucking maid and let's hit the sand."

"Top Gun time" described the alcohol-infused version of volleyball that we played, where elaborate high-five celebrations were just as important as points.

"I'll be out when I finish getting my shit set up," I told him.

He set two fresh beers down on my desk, looked over at me with disappointment, and said, "Don't be a bitch," then walked off down the hallway with his case of beer.

I finished making the bed, tossed my first empty can into the trash, and grabbed my drill out of the truck to mount my flat-screen on the wall. Every few minutes one of the guys would stop by and shoot the shit.

Rogers: Holy shit, Townes, I haven't seen you since the Fourth of July. Let's get fucking shitty tonight.

Monte: I am absolutely *dominating* v-ball. Come play on Team House Dogs when you're done.

Trendall: You're pretty ballsy letting Turbo be your neighbor.

Nate: Switch to whiskey. House dogs have a reputation to uphold.

Everyone living in the frat castle is known as a "house dog." It's a slogan that serves as a badge of honor and a label of responsibility to act even more demented than everyone else in the chapter, which is no easy task.

A few minutes later my room was in order, and I had finished off the beer Turbo left for me. I was making my way outside to toss a few boxes in the parking lot Dumpster when I felt my phone vibrating in my pocket. It was Monte, probably calling to hassle me about volleyball. I picked up and started talking immediately.

"Dude, I'm just tossing my boxes and then—"

"Get out here!" he interrupted. "Now! Turbo is about to light himself on fire!"

"What? Where?!"

I tossed the boxes into the Dumpster and took off running around the side of the house toward the backyard. When I turned the corner around the garden I saw Turbo in the volleyball pit sprinting back and forth along the net with a beer in one hand and a gasoline container in the other. He was singing at the top of his lungs and dousing the net with gas, spilling it all over the sand in the process.

"Highhhwaaay to the danger zone, dun dun dun dun! Gonna take it riiiight innnto the danger zone!"

Monte and I watched from a distance, amazed that within two hours of move-in he'd managed to black out *and* get his hands on a gas can. Trendall shook his head in disbelief and covered his eyes while the other guys who had been playing backed away from the court. I grabbed a beer from Turbo's cooler and leaned against our Civil War cannon to enjoy the show.

"House dogs!" screamed Turbo. "Let's play some fucking fireball!"

He slammed what was left of his beer, threw it straight up in the air, struck a match, and held it to the middle of what was clearly a brand-new net. Flames shot to the left and right, engulfing the entirety of the white twine. Turbo stumbled backwards, surprised by the size of his creation, tripped over the volleyball, and landed on his back with the gas canister still upright in his hand.

"Holy shit," he said under his breath.

The flames grew higher, giving off black smoke, and the net began to droop from damage, but Turbo got to his feet and picked up the volleyball, undeterred.

"All right, let's play! Let's see who's got the fucking nuts to try and spike it on me now!"

"Maybe you should take a few steps back from the flames," Trendall suggested.

Turbo's jaw tightened, his forehead wrinkled, and his excited smile wilted as he paced toward Trendall like he was going to hit him.

"I'm sick and tired of you being such a fucking pussy. Sand

doesn't burn. Now why don't you pull out your tampon and come—"

A piece of flaming twine fell from the net into the biggest gas puddle in the pit. With a *Wumph*, fire soared five feet into the air and a trail shot from one puddle to the next, causing a chain reaction of flames to run wild instantaneously. The biggest stream headed right for Turbo. He let out a high-pitched scream, dropped the gas canister, and dove out of the pit just as flames hit the spot where he had been standing and ran wild around the three-gallon container. When he hit the grass his left sandal was on fire, so he kicked and yelled in terror until it flew off into the yard.

The rank smell of burning rubber and twine mixed with the scent of gasoline as the net melted away in a blaze. Sunken pools of fire were scattered throughout the sand, and a thick cloud of smoke formed above the yard, trailing off into the sky. I took a sip of my beer and stared into the flames, abiding by the law of nature that man must be eternally obsessed with fire, as the blackened net crumbled to the ground.

"Well, that was fucking close!" Turbo yelled as he brushed himself off.

"Way to go, you fucking slapdick," said Monte. "Now how are we supposed to play?"

"Go buy us another net when the drugs wear off, you fucking pyro," Rogers said with annoyance.

"I'm not buying a fucking net! I pay my dues on time, which is more than anyone can say for you, Rogers."

As Turbo hurled rebuttals, the flames finally found their way into the gas container. It exploded in a compact blast that blew Turbo face first into the grass and rained sand down onto the patio. I instinctively ducked to my knees for cover, and

Trendall laughed with his head between his legs, basking in the fact that for once he was right to be paranoid.

The new president of Alpha, Taylor Ashcroft, sprinted out from inside the house with his hands in the air.

"What the hell is going on out here?"

I tore my gaze from the inferno that used to be our volleyball court and pointed to Turbo.

"God damn it, Turbo!" Ashcroft yelled. "What the hell?"

All he could do was shrug his shoulders.

We heard sirens in the distance, and the fire truck arrived within minutes.

Ashcroft sent everyone inside and assured the firemen that everything was okay while the rest of the chapter gathered in the kitchen to recount what had happened. Turbo told his version of the story again and again, which involved him dropping a match into the gas canister and hurling it onto the court, which didn't even make fucking sense. I watched through the window as the firemen reboarded their trucks and an enraged Ashcroft stormed back inside.

"Turbo!" he yelled, red-faced. "You're being fined $100 by the chapter, and if you don't have a new net up by tomorrow afternoon it will double. Don't ever fucking do something like this again."

As Ashcroft stomped up the stairs Turbo turned toward the group, smiling.

"Fuck the fine," he said. "It was worth it."

Volleyball was no longer an option, but everyone was fired up to be back on campus and living together at the house, so we decided some beer pong was in order. There were two rows of six solid wood tables that the '05 pledge class had constructed for times like these (and meals) in the dining room, so we grabbed a case from the fridge and headed in to rain some Ping-Pong balls. Monte and I were in the middle of a game against Parsells and Nate when Atwater strolled in.

"Those fucking Deltas next door are playing badminton in their front yard," he said with conviction. "Fucking *badminton*? Can you believe that?"

Our entire fraternity invariably loathed anything that the Deltas did. They were our biggest rivals on Greek Row, stemming from a feud in 1984 when they unsuccessfully attempted to steal our cannon from the backyard, resulting in a never-ending war of pranks, theft, and vandalism. It's impossible for hundreds of frat guys living on the same street to get along when they're trying to bang the same girls and sway the same rushees, but the Deltas' douchebaggery made the hatred exponentially worse. They were a bunch of try-hards who couldn't get into Alpha and spent the rest of their lives trying to convince themselves they were as cool as us.

"I'm so sick of their shit," said Nate.

"I bet it was them that called the fire department," Monte chimed in.

"Well, now we have to fuck with them," said Atwater, "and you have to explain why the hell the fire department was here."

"Wait a minute," said Nate. "I've got a bag of water balloons and a launcher in my room."

We dropped the Ping-Pong balls and headed straight for his room, which shared a bathroom with Monte's. Nate strapped the first balloon onto the sink to fill it up while Turbo, Atwater, Parsells, Monte, and I passed around a handle of whiskey and watched TV on his couch. I took a swig and had a sudden epiphany.

"Fuck shooting water at these guys. What are we, six-year-olds at a birthday party? Let's fill these things with piss."

The house had already begun to fill my head with destructive thoughts. It does things to a man's brain, like the hotel in *The Shining*. But no one questioned my idea, and thirty seconds later Nate had a balloon strapped to the tip of his dick as he leaned over his toilet and filled it with fluid.

"Damn, this thing is tight," he said. "It's cutting off the circulation."

"Don't lie, needle dick," said Monte. "You slide in there with room to spare."

Nate had to pull the balloon off before he was done relieving himself and splattered urine all over the floor as he tied it off. Then he went back to filling balloons with water in his sink while the rest of us took turns making piss balloons. One by one we all did the same thing, laughing as our morals streamed out of us.

When we were finished, Monte put the twenty water balloons and five urine balloons into a trash bag and we made our way up to the crow's nest, racing to get there first and snickering mischievously.

The top floor of the house was one giant empty room scattered with boxes of old textbooks and trash. The air was stale from lack of air-conditioning and cleaning. Some old composite photos from the 1970s were stacked in a corner with a file cabinet that served as the fraternity test bank, and wooden paddles etched with the names of generations of pledges were hung along the back wall. There were two doors; one was a closet filled with rotting old potatoes that we occasionally locked a pledge in, and the other led out onto the crow's nest.

I followed Monte to the crow's nest entrance and Turbo pushed me through with the five-foot rubber slingshot over his shoulder. We stumbled outside and took in a view of the entire campus.

As luck would have it, four Deltas were still playing badminton in their front yard while others watched in lawn chairs like the fucking posers that they were.

"Looks like they're having a nice little Saturday," said Monte as he loaded up the first regular water balloon.

Nate pulled his end of the slingshot tight, leaning himself up against the railing, while Turbo stretched the other end and leaned hard through the open door. Atwater, Parsells, and I ducked down and watched through the railing as Monte squatted and yanked the rubber back as far as he could. He quoted the movie *Gladiator* before releasing.

"At my signal, unleash hell."

Then he let the launcher loose and sent a balloon soaring into the evening air. It wobbled awkwardly down and slapped up against the fence between our yard and theirs. None of the Deltas even noticed.

"That was fucking pathetic," I said. "I could've thrown it that far."

I rustled around the trash bag, feeling for a cold balloon. It would be stupid to use a nice warm piss-filled one before we found our range. I placed it into the holster and took a three-second gulp of whiskey while I picked my target. Four of them were sitting around a table playing cards on the porch, so I took aim and pulled the rubber strap back as far as I could, dropping my weight down toward the ground to get a good angle.

"Whatever you do, don't be like Monte," said Atwater.

I released the cloth handle and the balloon launched out toward their yard, giving me an immediate appreciation for physics. I watched it cut through the air and could tell the trajectory was on point. A grin crept across my face as I squinted and tried to will it directly onto my target. It splattered in the middle of the table, sending cards flying everywhere.

Two of the Deltas jumped to their feet while the others wiped water from their brows, and they stared at their now empty table as cards fluttered down around them, trying to figure out what the hell was going on.

They peered around the yard, suspecting their own brothers as the attackers. Turbo tapped me on the shoulder and quickly loaded up another balloon. I pulled the launcher tight opposite Monte, and Turbo loosed his balloon in the direction of the badminton players. It nailed one of them in the back, causing him to jolt forward and drop his racket. He turned and looked up toward us.

"What the fuck is your problem?" he yelled.

"Go back to playing Indian tennis," Turbo yelled back. "You don't want to get hurt."

"I think it's time to send them a housewarming present," said Nate.

While Atwater and Turbo exchanged words with the Deltas, Monte and I readied the launcher and Nate loaded up a piss balloon. He launched it far and high into the air, and two of the Deltas skipped out of the way as it splattered on the porch pavement.

"Son of a bitch!" one of them yelled. "It's fucking piss!"

We all died laughing, and one of them hurled a full beer up at us, hitting the roof fifteen feet short.

"Nice throw, you fucking bitch!" yelled Turbo.

I loaded another piss balloon and sent it airborne. It landed flush on the left thigh of one of the card players.

"Motherfucker!" he yelled. "Get down here and I'll shove that slingshot up your fucking ass!"

He started walking toward our yard and six of his friends followed.

"You want to go?" Monte yelled. "Let's fucking go!"

I grabbed the bag of balloons and the five of us hauled ass down to the first floor as fast as we could, jumping down the staircases. When we got to the front door and opened it the Deltas were standing in the yard yelling obscenities and throwing beer cans. I quickly handed everyone a balloon from the bag and we ran into the yard, pelting them while they tried to dodge our assault.

I nailed a stumpy kid with brown hair in the face as hard as I could, and he ran toward me, diving for a tackle. I stiff-armed him on the top of the head, pushing his face into the grass, and grabbed another balloon to peg him in the back. Monte spear-tackled the biggest guy in the yard, and Turbo danced around one of them with a balloon in hand yelling, "This one is filled with warm piss! Do you want it? Do you want it?"

I noticed a group of four sorority girls stopped in the street, watching in awe, and that's when a Delta named Steve threw the first punch.

Nate took it square in the jaw and reeled backward. I tackled Steve to the ground and started throwing haymakers into his stomach.

"Fuck you, Townes!" he yelled.

"Suck my dick, Steve, you pouty bitch!" I reared back and hit him square in the right cheek.

The next thing I knew Rogers and Ashcroft were pulling me off Steve as a police siren sounded in the street. We scattered like cockroaches. The Deltas sprinted back onto their property and we retreated into the house.

Atwater, Rogers, Turbo, and I regrouped in Monte's room and made fun of Nate for getting cold-cocked.

"I can't believe you let that ass pirate hit you in the face," said Atwater, panting to catch his breath. "I have political science with that kid and he's a fucking joke."

"I didn't *let* him hit me, dickhead. It just happened."

"I returned the favor," I said, cracking the aching knuckles on my right hand.

A few minutes later Ashcroft walked in rubbing his temples, and we all stopped talking and looked innocently up at him.

"Look," he said. "The cops just told me if there's *one* more incident tonight they *have* to give us a ticket for something. Please, *please* try and keep it under control. I don't want to get a phone call from nationals asking why five of our guys got arrested on move-in day. You know we're having a party in a couple hours, right? We don't need any more heat! Just! Stop!"

Nate tried to explain.

"Ashcroft, the fucker hit me in—"

"JUST! STOP!" Ashcroft rolled his eyes and stormed out of the room.

"All right, all right, Jesus," said Nate. "I miss when Harvey was president. He would've been in there throwing punches with us."

"Speaking of tonight's party," Turbo chimed in. "It's time to pregame. Who's down to finish up that beer pong?"

Ashcroft could yell all he wanted, but there was nothing he could do to stop our momentum. The first night of the fall semester was always one of the wildest. Everyone had been either been cooped up back home with their families, taking summer school, or working, and they needed to let the bad out, so the five of us headed back to the dining room to continue doing just that.

Monte and I got in a couple games against Nate and Rogers, and I was watching Atwater and Turbo set up for a mega-sized game with forty cups when I felt a deep rumble in my stomach. It was my blackout radar reminding me that I hadn't eaten anything since breakfast on the way into town. If I was going to make it through the imminent party I needed some fuel to keep me going.

I convinced Monte to drive to Jack in the Box, and we ordered enough food for a family of five. I inhaled four 99-cent tacos, two hamburgers, and a box of cheese sticks in five minutes, much to the delight of two teenagers watching in awe from the table next to us. On the ride home I felt like a man renewed, saved again by the power of the blackout radar I had finely tuned through years of drinking experience starting back in high school.

We arrived back at the frat castle to a packed parking lot, with several guys unloading the last boxes of liquor from the bed of Scott McCandles's truck. McCandles was the current social chair, and when the social chair showed up with the beer and liquor it meant it was time for the fun to start. Girls were already roaming the street to see which parties were getting under way, and I sent a mass text to every worthy female in my phone to make absolutely sure they knew we were ready to rumble: PARTY AT ALPHA NOW.

The way I figured it, now that we'd eaten a meal and taken a break from drinking, Monte and I were behind, so we headed to my room and I filled a beer bong three-fourths with beer and one-fourth with whiskey and handed it to him.

"You first, big fella."

He sucked it down and gagged, but managed to finish it off. I was up next and he made the same mixture for me. I took it down in three gulps, coughing as I pulled it away from my lips.

I was washing the taste out with the last of my Sprite from our fast-food trip when Nate busted through the door with a look of excitement on his face.

"Some GDI just crashed his longboard into the telephone pole in the front yard! He's cut up pretty bad!"

As my stomach grumbled the three of us ran out to the front yard, and I immediately spotted the injured geed sitting on the curb being tended to by Atwater and Turbo. If there was a combination of two people I wanted taking care of me during a time of injury, they were not it. The geed's left cheek was scraped with road rash, and blood was trickling down his neck as he held his knee and panicked.

"I caught too much speed coming down that fucking hill," said the geed. His eyes filled with tears.

Atwater played doctor and wiped the blood away from a three-inch gash on his shin.

"It's pretty fucking deep, buddy. Can you stand?"

"I can barely bend it," he said.

"Well, me and Turbo here will carry you up to the house so you can wait inside for an ambulance," said Atwater.

I grabbed the injured kid's backpack and we headed back up toward the house. Nate and I took a seat on the porch bench while Atwater and Turbo went to wash the geed up, and as the whiskey-beer bong started to sink in I noticed Nate unzipping the backpack.

"What the hell are you doing?" I asked.

Nate ignored me, dropped his shorts, sat on the porch railing, and held the backpack behind him underneath his bare ass.

"Nate, what the fuck?"

"Sometimes you've got to pay the piper, Townes," he said.

I turned away as he dropped a steaming log into the poor bastard's backpack.

"Dude, you can't give that guy a fucking backpack filled with your shit," I yelled at him. "Obviously he's going to know it was us."

"You're right, Townes," he said. "This is fucked up and we have to get rid of it."

He picked up the backpack and hurled it over the porch into the Deltas' yard, smirking at me.

"There. Problem solved."

I stared at him in shock as he walked inside the house, totally indifferent to the situation he had just created. The ambulance rolled up while I sat with my mouth agape in complete disbelief, and I decided I didn't want to be there when the poor guy started asking what happened to his bag, so I quickly headed around the back of the house to join the party.

McCandles and his party committee had set up two shot blocks on the basketball court, which are 240-pound blocks of ice with grooves carved from the top to the bottom. They rest at an angle on wooden platforms so that liquor can be poured down the grooves. The ice makes the liquor so cold that you barely taste it as it slides down your throat. There was already a group of girls in line as Rogers and Trendall dumped Jäger down the slides and into their mouths.

I made my way through the growing crowd and ran into a

group of Omega girls. One of them, named Lacey, had gone on Spring Break with us to Puerto Vallarta and we had made out a few times, but I never closed the deal. Seeing the dark direction that the night was already headed in, I decided I no longer needed to be a part of the party and there was no better time than now to finish what I'd started on Spring Break.

"Lacey, how was your summer?" I asked.

"It was great! I spent a month in Costa Rica studying abroad. I've missed you, though! Did you move in today?"

"I did, actually. Wanna go take shots in my room?"

"You know I do."

We headed to my room and took shots of vodka while she told me about Costa Rica, and then she grabbed my high school photo album off my desk and we looked through it together sitting on my bed. When she leaned into me to point at a picture of me on my high school baseball team, the sexual tension grew and I tilted her chin with my index finger and pressed my lips into hers. I pulled away from her slowly, nonchalantly stood up, closed my door, and locked it.

"I was hoping you'd do that," she said.

We made out for a few minutes, and when I started a battle with the button on her shorts she reached down and stopped me.

"You're going to hate me," she said. "It's that time of the month."

"Ohhh...well, I understand," I said. "No reason to feel bad. I'm pretty sure I don't hate you."

"Well, let me make absolutely sure," she said as she rolled me on my side and straddled me.

She ripped my belt from my shorts and pulled them down with her teeth. All I could do was sit back and enjoy the show.

It turned out Lacey gave the best damn blowjob I had ever gotten. She finished me off so fast that I felt like I had been robbed. Afterwards she washed her mouth out in the bathroom, kissed me on the cheek, and said goodbye. The "fish in a barrel" analogy didn't even do the frat castle justice.

It was only 1:45 a.m., but I was so satisfied, full of food, and still hammered that I couldn't even bring myself to rejoin the party. I figured there was no way I was going to improve upon that ending to my first night in the house anyway, so I made sure my bathroom and bedroom door were both locked so that Turbo wouldn't come in later and fuck with me, and slipped into a deep, peaceful sleep.

———

Most guys just go to the house to party, and don an entirely new attitude of arrogance while they're there. But when you live in the house, that attitude becomes a lifestyle, and the drinking never stops. The parties are one thing, but it's the ridiculous shit that goes on outside those parties that most people never get to experience. It's something you have to live to truly understand, but these TFMs will help...

On Living at the Fraternity House

Telling fat chicks that the frat castle is at capacity. TFM.

Our neighbors listen to awesome music, whether they like it or not. TFM.

The chimney at the house is filled to the top with beer cans from roof drinking. TFM.

Walked past three bathrooms in the frat castle to piss off the balcony. TFM.

It's not illegal if it happens in the frat house. TFM.

Getting an awkward stare from your neighbors because you brought home a screamer last night. TFM.

Our fraternity house has his/her bathrooms and co-ed showers. TFM.

The house is a combination of a country club, a brothel, and a Chevy dealership. TFM.

The phrase "hold my beer" leading to a trip to the ER. TFM.

"Wanna go take shots in my room?" TFM.

Stand-up doggie in the frat house stall. TFM.

The morning struggle between "too hungover to get up"
and "if I don't get a drink of water I'm going to die." TFM.

Backup doors, because you'll need them. TFM.

Safety is never first. TFM.

The self-loathing house manager. TFM.

The frat castle roof is the 19th tee. TFM.

Slip 'n slide at the house. TFM.

The Tailgate

WHEN DONE RIGHT, TAILGATING FOR COLLEGE FOOTBALL offers a unique scenario in which a young scholar can display many outstanding qualities: godlike alcohol tolerance, insensitivity to the personal space of others, the ability to throw a tight-spiraled football and showcase superior genetics, and a wardrobe that would make JFK feel like a goth. During my sophomore year, preceding the biggest game of the season against our rival, I turned in my finest tailgating performance. The following is a chronology of events on that game day.

7 a.m. Somewhere in the house, someone cracks a Keystone. The sound echoes through the silent halls like a gunshot. That first beer is the starter pistol for the entire house of alcoholics to start binging.

7:01 a.m. Adrenaline for the biggest football day of the year is tingling in my balls, and I spring out of bed to join whoever has already begun the process of getting game-day drunk. Kickoff is at 2:30 p.m., but if you aren't tailgating with a solid buzz by 9 a.m., you're a fucking rookie.

7:05 a.m. I enter my bathroom and discover Pledge Yates seated on my toilet. I laugh as I remember drunkenly ordering him to be on my toilet at 6:50 a.m. sharp to make sure the seat is warm for my morning dump. He is the Porcelain Pledge.

7:20 a.m. After aggressively relieving myself, I gear up in my finest school pride apparel to join the group of early-rising boozers on the front porch. Brooks Brothers tie, matching pants, blazer, and loafers. I'm fucking handsome. As I exit my room I can smell the house chef's eggs and bacon.

7:25 a.m. I sip my first beer on the porch as someone's slampiece wearing men's basketball shorts, a large date party T-shirt, and high heels scurries out of the house past me on her way off the property. I reflexively rate her a 7 on a scale of 1–10. Turbo starts a "WALK OF SHAME!" chant and we keep it going until her car pulls out of the parking lot.

7:27 a.m. I crack open beer no. 2.

7:28 a.m. Another unfortunate girl exits the house, this time jogging and holding her heels. She is beat. I rate her a 4. She knows what's coming and attempts to cover her ears as she runs by our group of hecklers, so our "WALK OF SHAME!" chant turns into a chorus of boos after a few rounds.

7:32 a.m. Eight of us circle up on the porch and I shotgun beer no. 3. The day has officially begun. Beer drips down my chin as I spike my empty can to the ground.

7:35 a.m. I notice a group of our pledges arriving in a fleet of trucks. They are returning from setting up the tent, satellite, televisions, beer pong tables, couches, and chairs at our reserved tailgate area outside the stadium. Now they will be serving our breakfast.

7:36 a.m. I crack open beer no. 4.

7:37 a.m. I throw empty beer no. 4 at a pledge as he walks past me into the house.

7:38 a.m. I crack open beer no. 5.

7:55 a.m. I pour my first mimosa in the dining room as a pledge waiter sets my breakfast in front of me. My plate is covered in eggs and seven strips of crispy bacon. I slosh champagne-spiked orange juice around in my mouth and the sound of our university fight song fills the room as brothers and coeds file in to feast and drink. In my book, they're fucking late.

8:10 a.m. The room is packed with over seventy people clad in game-day attire. We are an eating, breathing, drinking mob of sports fan greatness, ready to join tens of thousands of others on the concrete tailgate battlefield.

8:30 a.m. Two mimosas later, the alcohol in my system from last night's rager has combined with this morning's intake to skyrocket my BAC above the legal driving limit. At this hour on a normal day that would make me one of the most pathetic degenerates in America, but today it makes me a fucking war machine of school pride.

8:40 a.m. I head outside to get in line for the bus.

8:45 a.m. I high-five our regular bus driver, Frank, on my way up the bus steps and immediately grab a fresh cold one from one of the five coolers on board. Frank gives my drinking habits a nod of respect.

8:50 a.m. Turbo and I are hanging out the bus windows yelling obnoxiously at every girl we pass. "Hey girl, you want your first baby to have a trust fund?" hollers Turbo. A girl in a floral dress takes particular offense and shoots him a nasty glare after he shouts, "Pull up that flower dress and show off those stems!"

9 a.m. The bus parks and we bust through the rear emergency exit doors instead of waiting in line to go out the front. The air is filled with the smell of cigarettes, barbecue, fresh-cut grass, and American freedom.

9:05 a.m. I scan the horizon and head straight toward our fraternity flag, which is waving proudly just below Old Glory on the flagpole at our tent. The flag serves as the North Star when I'm sailing blackout drunk through the sea of tailgate tents.

9:07 a.m. The five-minute break between the bus and our tent gives my liver the only chance it will have all day to catch its breath. Unfortunately, my lungs are not so lucky. I drunkenly demand a cigarette from a stranger, and suck it down like the last drops of a milkshake.

9:10 a.m. I throw in a man-sized dip and take in the 75 degrees of sunshine. Perfect football weather. There is no fucking way we lose.

9:30 a.m. Tailgate is in full swing. I win my first game of beer pong and celebrate with a beer bong.

9:45 a.m. I win my second game of beer pong and celebrate with a beer bong.

9:46 a.m. I take my talents to the washer boards to dominate the old balls seniors with Turbo. Some neighboring tailgaters who are obviously prominent alumni are staring at us with concern as we stomp along to "Wagon Wheel," yelling every word at the top of our lungs.

9:50 a.m. I glare around the crowd looking for anyone wearing colors that could resemble the visiting team's. I spot a lone enemy in our opponent's gear weaving through the crowd under the tent next to ours.

9:51 a.m. I jump up on a couch, point at the enemy with authority, and yell, "You're going down, sheep-fucker!"

9:52 a.m. An empty beer can flies out of our tailgate and clanks off the enemy's right shoulder. He shakes his head and flees, defeated.

9:53 a.m. Police officers warn us that they will shut down our tailgate if we attack visiting fans.

9:54 a.m. Our fight song is turned on, and our tent erupts into a chorus of cheers, high fives, and fist bumps. I take out my dip and throw it at a passing pledge. It sticks to his chest.

9:55 a.m. I rummage through the ice in our biggest Yeti cooler, searching for another beer, but pull out a handle of McCormick vodka. I hold it and debate whether or not to take a pull. I consider the fact that some total hottie who gets super wet when guys chug vodka could be watching, and she'd be turned off if I just put it down. I unscrew the cap, take a huge swig, and vomit into the cooler as I drop the handle back in and slam the lid closed.

9:56 a.m. I wipe my chin with a paper towel. It seems no one has noticed my contribution to the cooler. I stumble to another cooler and grab an American Bud to wash the taste of vomit from my mouth.

10:10 a.m. I lean against the hot dog table to support myself, totally shitfaced and loving every second of it. Monte strolls up to the tailgate, now hours late by my standards. He is as sober as a priest, yapping away in my face, but I can't understand a fucking word he's saying because I'm too busy trying to process the fact that the game is still four hours away.

10:20 a.m. "Turbo, give me some fucking Adderall. I know you have some. I need it."

10:21 a.m. I fold the Adderall up in a napkin and crush it up by hitting it repeatedly with the back of my iPhone. Then I unfold the napkin, lean down, and snort it. My nostrils burn as Turbo repeatedly tugs an imaginary train horn and chugs his beer in excitement. He knows the animal inside me is about to be unleashed, and he's ready to embrace it.

11 a.m. The Porcelain Pledge regretfully fulfills his obligation to obey me as an active and prepares yet another beer bong for me. He can judge me, but there's nothing he can do to stop me. I am Hurricane Townes.

11:45 a.m. A freshman Zeta is pulled away from me by her big sister, who tells me I need to calm down and sober up. I yell, "I got here at nine o'clock, damn it!" as they walk away, but they don't seem to understand. All the Adderall has done is increase the rate at which I slur.

12:30 p.m. A police officer orders me to relax after I flip a couch following a beer pong win.

12:35 p.m. Alcohol has eaten through the eggs, bacon, and hot dogs I've consumed, and I am now a walking zombie of debauchery.

12:45 p.m. I am tongue deep with the solid 4 who left the house to a chorus of boos this morning. I know it's her, and I don't care.

12:50 p.m. I throw in another man-sized dip.

1 p.m. I spot another visiting fan two tents over. I grab the football from Monte, who was playing catch with a pledge, and hurl it as hard as I can at the outsider douchebag's head. It sails through the air in a perfect spiral, and then hits the kid standing next to my target. He spills his beer all over the guy I was aiming at. I duck behind a couch.

1:20 p.m. I take another shotgun to the face as people chant, "TOWNES! TOWNES! TOWNES!" around me. I spike the can as they cheer, realize I just swallowed my dip, stumble out from under the tent, climb into the back of a pledge's truck, and throw up in the bed.

1:35 p.m. I exit the truck bed and see that people are finally making their way toward the stadium. I stumble in the mob's direction, but out of the corner of my eye I see a group of guys clad in the other team's colors throwing their empty beers and hot dog wrappers on the ground under our tent. One of them has both middle fingers pointed directly at me, and I hear him say, "Hope you're ready to lose, you white trash fuck." With a running start I barrel-roll over a couch, knock over a trash can, and clothesline the fucker with perfect Hulk Hogan form.

1:36 p.m. Two of his friends attempt to pull me off him as I give him a vicious noogie, and one of them lands a shot on the back of my head before several Alphas break it up. They restrain me and throw me into the back of the puke truck just before police arrive to investigate. Pledge Danna tells me to lie down, climbs into the driver's seat, and hits the gas.

1:37 p.m. As Pledge Danna navigates intense game-day traffic, I drunkenly try to position myself so that none of the throw-up in the bed of his truck touches me.

1:40 p.m. I pass out in the fetal position at a red light with my cheek against the cold, yack-covered steel.

9:45 p.m. I come to in the bed of a random truck parked in the fraternity house lot. I immediately realize I've missed the game. It looks like people are drinking on the back porch.

9:50 p.m. I crack open beer no. 1.

———

College football provides an atmosphere unlike any other sport in the world. Tailgates are planned weeks before the season even starts, and wild amounts of money are invested in season tickets, tents, grills, attire, and alcohol. In big-time college towns the entire city embraces the tradition and shows up in full force along with students, alumni, and faculty. These TFMs represent this phenomenon in all its glory...

On College Football Tailgating

We dress like we're going to church on game days, because this is God's country. TFM.

Purebred black lab puppy at tailgate. It's like fishing with dynamite. TFM.

Perfecting the one-handed-football-catch-without-spilling-my-beer move. TFM.

Good luck kicking me out of this tailgate. My granddad's name is on the stadium. TFM.

If my life were a football game there would be a lot of excessive celebration penalties. TFM.

Blacked out at noon for the 5:30 game, came to singing the National Anthem in the stadium. TFM.

Slapping a flat brim off a GDI during the National Anthem. TFM.

Being at the game, but still having to watch the highlights to see what happened. TFM.

Yes, I do stand throughout the whole football game. Yes, I do wait for the band to play the alma mater after the game. Yes, I do sing the Star Spangled Banner. No, I do not remember any of it. TFM.

4½ year plan just for one more football season. TFM.

Blazers and shorts. TFM.

Asserting dominance during tailgate. TFM.

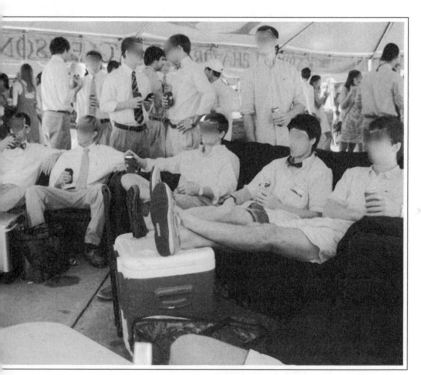

Watching the big screen at tailgate. TFM.

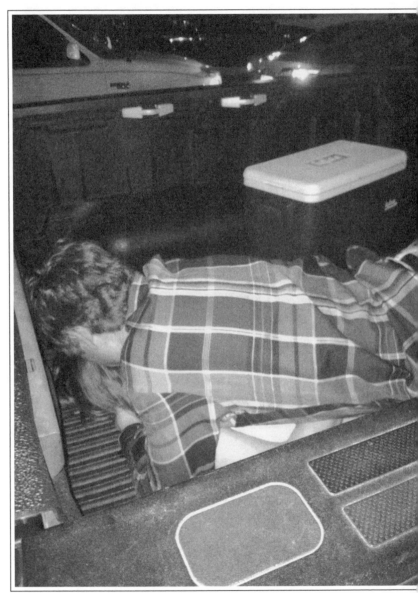

The post-tailgate hookup. TFM.

Popping bottles. TFM.

Sorostitute Stories

IN HIGH SCHOOL, GETTING LAID WAS LIKE LEARNING a foreign language. It took a lot of time, a lot of effort, and was difficult as fuck to master. Convincing girls to participate in an act that parents, teachers, and doctors have painted in a negative light since they were old enough to understand is no easy task. As guys, the deck was completely stacked against us and opportunities were few and far between, but when those girls waved bye-bye to their parents, teachers, and doctors, the game changed.

With the freedom of college came an entirely different outlook. Everyone was fucking. Campus was basically a sex commune. Every night the BAC of the student body took a sharp turn upward and the odds of getting a girl in bed improved dramatically for even the most unsightly scholars. This was even truer for those of us fortunate enough to be members of upstanding Greek organizations with tilted moral compasses and a never-ending supply of alcohol.

Four specific experiences took me through the progressive stages of my own sexual awakening during school, each of which was important for different reasons. They made me who I am today, and without them I'd just be another clueless idiot thrusting away with a girl who deserves better and is just hoping it will end soon.

Stage 1: Busch League

As a freshman on a campus filled with morally loosened girls, I had no idea how to handle the clashing lifestyles of binge drinking and sexual promiscuity. That quickly became clear with Allison and the cannon incident during rush, and my failure to bang Amy on bid night, but I got better as I went and had my successes with girls like Lacey at the frat castle. There was plenty of opportunity to gain experience and become a drunken intercourse artist, because everyone in college parties for the same reason: to get ass. The alcohol was really just mental lubricant.

By the spring of my freshman year I was so used to closing on girls that if I didn't end up back in my bed post-party with a 7 or better I considered the night a failure. It had even become the norm to get some mid-party action, like a dance floor over-the-pants handjob (OTPHJ).

In the middle of a spring rush party at the Alpha house, I ended up in a heated sexual dance-off with a girl named Britney. She was a skinny, tan, blonde Kappa and I badly needed to tap that. After locking eyes across the crowded dance floor she wiggled her way over to me, and just a few songs later we stumbled out the door toward my dorm.

Like the Karate Kid before Mr. Miyagi, I lacked experience, but possessed raw talent. We were both freshmen, we were both shitfaced, and we both wanted something good to tell our friends the next day. After she finished a few minutes of dry handjob pumping during a makeout session with too much tongue, she slid off her thong and said, "You can if you want," with one eyebrow raised and an innocent smile on her face.

"I can what?" I asked like the complete fucking dumbass I am.

"You know..." she said playfully.

I looked deep into her eyes and said, "You're the girl I came to college to find."

She flung her thong across the room and pulled me on top of her by the back of my head. I awkwardly poked my dick around between her legs as her eyes widened with anticipation, and finally she reached down to guide me inside. A quick mental note was filed away in my brain that she was not only girl no. 4 to feel little Townes inside her, but also that she was my first Kappa. Knowing that I'd gained another belt-notch of bragging rights and checked a new sorority off my list made me swell with pride both literally and figuratively. She felt it, and smiled up at me in contentment, which caused me to totally lose my cool, and I immediately started jackhammering away like a rabbit having an epileptic seizure.

I squeezed her right boob like a stress ball with one hand while the other rested on the bed, awkwardly close to her left hand, and as she inched her fingers closer to mine I could tell she wanted me to hold it. She moaned, arched her back, and whispered my name, sending my heart rate through the roof and increasing the speed of my humping. I made eye contact with her for a second, and awkwardly looked away as fast as possible, which I immediately regretted.

I was running my train full speed ahead down the tracks with no brakes. There was no fucking way I was switching positions. This was a straight missionary onslaught. She sighed with pleasure, grabbed my ass hard with both hands, and started moaning my name loudly in my ear.

"TOWNES! TOWNES!"

I desperately tried to think of something hot to say, but drew a blank. Then "It feels really good" rushed out of my mouth before my brain had a chance to process how stupidly honest that sounds.

I put both my hands above her shoulders and locked my arms out, basically in push-up position, giving myself a solid view of her boobs as they bounced from my super-speed pelvic humping, and conveniently distancing myself from her non-stop shrieking of my name.

"TOWNES! TOWNES! TOWNES!" she yelled.

I was getting close to a penile volcanic eruption, so I tried to occupy my mind by reciting the presidents of the United States I could remember. She must've been able to feel me getting close, because she looked me in the eye and whispered sweetly, "Make sure you pull out." I was trying to time my exit and hold the money shot as long possible with my remembrance of American history when, at the exact same second I got to Reagan on my list of presidents, Monte drunkenly stumbled in the door. "Daddy is home!" he yelled right as Britney slapped my ass. I erupted like Mount Vesuvius inside her, awkwardly staring over at Monte with a look of horror on my face while I came. I frantically pulled out and rolled over off her, but the damage was done.

"God damn it, Townes, that's not okay!" she yelled. "Fucking idiot!"

She pushed me off her and started dabbing herself with my bedsheet like that was going to fix anything. Monte slurred, "Well, that was fucking weird," and passed out face first on his bed. I sat up, awkwardly squished up against the wall, and tried to apologize to Britney, but she didn't want to hear it and walked to the bathroom to clean up.

When she got back she shook her head and said, "Do you know how lucky you are that I'm on birth control?" before kissing me on the cheek and rolling over to sleep. I lay next to her with one arm folded behind my head, too satisfied with how fucking awesome the night was to occupy my mind with the fact that my performance was totally Busch League. If I could spend every night like this but it had to end with Monte busting in as I crossed the finish line, I would be okay with that.

That's when I knew I was a rookie in the game of sexual dominance, and the learning had only just begun.

Stage 2: Overcoming Obstacles

After a camo-themed mixer during the fall of my sophomore year, I ended up inside the Tri Delt house with a blonde senior who had legs like a runway model. Spending the night inside a sorority house was like breaking into a fucking casino vault. Even if you managed to sneak in without security or the house mom noticing, you still had to avoid all the other girls in the house on the way to her bedroom, because one of those cock-blocking gossip queens was bound to rat you out. This girl was hot as fuck, and twenty-one years old. This story was already worthy of sharing at my next chapter meeting before it even developed.

Too bad I couldn't remember her name. I was at least fourteen drinks and 20 millis of Adderall deep, so my brain and dick were in full mutiny against me. *Is it Kimmy? Kristen?* My mind raced as I took her pants off with one hand and tried to wake my dick up with the other. Adderall-dick is a real problem with no known cure.

It was 3:45 a.m. and my face was painted like Charlie Sheen's in *Platoon*. I was wearing a camouflage bandana around my forehead, and combat boots. That was all. She was as naked as the day she was born, with black and green stripes painted up and down both arms, and eye black, which was smudged down her face thanks to alcohol and party sweat. She was a smoking-hot drunk 8, probably a sober 7, but even as she orally embraced my balls I couldn't remember her damn name.

My epic battle with whiskey/Adderall dick continued. We silently strategized what to try next with sign language as she repeatedly reminded me with one finger across her lips that I had to be quiet so we wouldn't wake up her roommate. For the better part of a half hour I struggled valiantly, switching between receiving a seriously impressive blowie from this incredibly understanding woman and thwacking my soft dong between her legs in search of an entryway. She had obviously dealt with her fair share of beer penis over the years, and was pulling out all the stops to make absolutely sure she got laid. Even on blowjob attempt no. 4 she hadn't lost a bit of her energy.

As she violently bobbed her head, desperate to breathe life back into my dick, I considered telling her to stop and throwing in the towel. That's when I looked over and noticed her roommate lying on her side in bed, watching us. And she wasn't just watching, she was staring right at me and licking her lips with a look that sent shivers through my entire body, instantly causing me to become rock hard. She had just done what science had failed to do since the dawn of Adderall.

How I had managed to stumble into the room dressed like a wasted G.I. Joe and not even take a glance at the insanely attractive brunette sleeping in the bed just a few feet away is beyond me. To my knowledge I'd never had anyone watch me hook up, but apparently I loved it. The girl whose mouth my manhood currently inhabited and whose name I had forgotten gave a moan of approval. I snapped into action, threw her legs over my shoulders, and slid home. This was the most turned on I had ever been in my life.

She wrapped her legs around me and I looked back over at the roommate, who was sucking her middle finger like a Popsicle. She switched to her pointer finger, then ran them both slowly down her stomach below the sheets. In my completely smashed state of mind I wondered if it was possible that I had created the roommate in some alcohol/amphetamine hallucination, and if I should invite the possible mirage sorosty to join in. I looked down at the girl I was inside of, and she started to turn her head, presumably to check if her roommate was awake. I grabbed her by the chin and kissed her to keep her focus on me. She grabbed for one of her pillows and pressed it to her face, moaning into it as I stroked away while never breaking my wide-eyed staredown with the roommate as she bit her bottom lip and fingered herself.

After a couple minutes I flipped her over into doggie style and she put her face back into the pillow to stay quiet. Her sexy-ass roommate was squeezing her tits with one hand while the other kept busy beneath the sheet. My dick had reached diamond status, and Kristen (?) thought it was all because of her. I winked at her roommate, and she shivered noticeably, aggressively sliding her other hand beneath the sheet as well.

I was laying some serious pipe, with one hand on each of

her hips pulling her back into me. She seemed to be enjoying the position, and I turned to check on her roommate again. The possibly crazy nympho was now completely uncovered and shamelessly touching herself with both knees up and her toes curled down. She stared into my eyes again, her mouth agape with pleasure as she worked her fingers faster and faster toward orgasm, and she was taking me right along with her.

But without warning, the girl whose name I was pretty sure started with a K turned and caught her roommate staring at me and masturbating.

"Danielle, what the fuck!" She pushed me off her, pulling the covers over us both. "Ughhhh, why do you always do this?" she yelled up at the ceiling. "I'm sorry, Jim," she groaned in disgust.

"Who the hell is Jim?" I asked. "I'm Townes." She ignored me.

I looked over at the roommate, but to my disappointment she had rolled over and was pretending to be asleep.

"Look, Townes, you should probably go," she said. "I'm really sorry, but it's just better if you just go."

"Yeah, uh, we should do this again," I said as I pulled my camo pants up over my throbbing boner.

On the way out of the house I gave zero fucks if anyone saw me or not. I whistled as I strolled down the hallway and passed one girl coming out of the restroom in her night slip. She rolled her eyes at me and ducked back into the bathroom to wait until I passed. I couldn't help but laugh to myself as the experience sunk in, and I made my way down the stairs to the exit. Could I have pulled off the threesome if I'd played my cards right? I would never know. The house's alarm beeped twice as I walked out, and then I slammed the door as hard as

I could to purposely cause some middle-of-the-night sorority drama.

I still had a lot to learn.

Stage 3: Finding Mr. Miyagi

It was Spring Break in Panama City my junior year. I was twenty. She was nineteen and went to Ole Miss. We obviously both had great fake IDs, and after we locked eyes at the bar I walked over to her.

"I'm Townes, and those guys you're with are complete douchebags."

"I'm not really with them," she said. "My friends already went home to crash. I'm Kelli."

"Well, Kelli, you should come drink with me and my friends. We're not douchebags and we don't wear sparkly Ed Hardy shirts, plus we have a hot tub."

An hour later we were getting out of a cab in front of my house, where everyone else was already passed out or slamming in their respective rooms. Three minutes after that she was pulling her skintight dress off and getting into the hot tub wearing black boy-shorts and a red-laced bra that screamed, *I knew someone would fuck my brains out tonight.* She had long brown hair and the kind of tits that cause flat, jealous girls to beg their dad for a boob job. I was wearing boxers covered in little sailboats that screamed, *I'm in a frat, play with my dick.*

After a few fun rounds of slap-the-bag wine chugging and some flirty touching, I went in for the kill. Immediately I could tell that this girl knew what she was doing. She wasn't making out with me like it was a fun drunk hookup; she was making out with me like it was the apocalypse, the world was crumbling around us, and she intended to go out with a bang. She straddled me, took off her bra, and let it sink away beneath the bubbling hot water. I buried my face in her chest and she grabbed the bag of wine off the hot tub, slapped it, and took a mouthful while I motorboated her fantastic boobage. At that moment I wanted to marry her.

Then she took it to a whole other level.

"Are you ready for this?" she asked as she handed me the bag of wine.

"Born ready," I responded without any idea what I was in store for.

The next thing I knew she was submerged, ripped my boxers off, and started performing the greatest amateur underwater fellatio in the history of man. I did the only thing I could do and took a swig of wine to keep my brain from short-circuiting due to sensory overload. Her legs floated up behind her as she passionately worked but somehow never came up for air. I had become a human snorkel.

A minute passed as I sat in pleasure with my jaw dropped. King Henry VIII would've decapitated all the women in England for that treatment. She came up for a quick oxygen refill gasp and then went back under without a word. Another minute passed and I saw her black boy-shorts float up next to me. I don't even know how, but she took off her fucking undies without losing blowjob rhythm...all while underwater.

In one fluid motion she resurfaced and pounced, wrapping her legs around me like a sexual spider monkey. She started riding me like she had been training for that moment her entire life while watching all of Shakira's music videos on repeat. This girl knew things, things that I needed to learn, and I intended on letting her teach me.

She leaned forward to my ear and whispered, "Bend me over." I obliged. Then she turned her head back and said, "Pull my hair." I was in heaven. For at least a half hour she whispered commands and I willfully obeyed like a good student should.

"Fuck me faster." *Bam. Bam. Bam.*

"Spank me, Daddy." *Hell yeah, you're a bad girl.*

"Put your finger in my ass." *Sweet.*

"Pour wine down my chest and drink it off." *Thank you, Jesus.*

"Choke me." *Why not?*

"Harder!" *Please don't die.*

"Slap me." *Forgive me, Jesus.*

"Bend me over the balcony." *Done.*

"Let's fuck on the beach." *Time to get sandy.*

We both grabbed towels, headed down the stairs, and stumbled toward the beach, sloppily making out the whole hundred yards. When we were close to the ocean she jumped onto my back and wrapped her legs around me, sending us both to the sand. She unwrapped the towel from my waist and started riding me reverse cowgirl, screaming toward the ocean while I stared up at the stars and wondered if life would ever be this good again. When I couldn't take it anymore I flipped her around and got on top of her to complete the manifesto. I pulled out when I was about to finish so I could make a little castle on the sand, but she gave me one last whisper.

"Go on my face."

Afterwards we washed off in the ocean and headed back to the house, where we sat in two beach chairs on the porch, shared half a joint she had in her purse, and watched the sun come up. I had broken through to a new level of sexual illumination.

Stage 4: Showing Off Enlightenment

It was the fall of my first senior year, and I was at J's Piano Bar, a favorite of the Greek community. I ran into a psychotic ex-slam from my second semester named Katherine. We broke up after she ransacked my room, keyed my car, and blew a senior because she accused me of dancing with one of her sisters during a foam party. She was in her third consecutive long-term relationship with a bottom-tier douchebag. I decided this was as good a time as any to make a run at her, because I was wasted, the piano man was playing "Piano Man," and her boyfriend, bottom-tier Billy, was nowhere to be seen.

"We're having a huge after-party at the frat castle. You in?"

She naughtily raised one eyebrow and said, "Sure, I'll come by for a little."

"Awesome." I smiled seductively at her. "It's been too long since we hung out."

Thirty minutes later we were up against the wall in the frat castle hallway and she was trying to suck my tongue out of my mouth. She thought she was just cheating her way onto the same dick she knew years ago, but I was about to put on a fucking clinic.

We vertically barrel-rolled down the hall wall while I tried not to spill my beer until we hit my door. I turned the knob and Katherine fell in onto my floor. She laughed, I laughed, and then I decided to let her know it was game time. I picked her up and threw her onto my bed like a Viking warrior claiming his bride, then chugged what was left of my beer and spiked it to the floor. She gazed up at me like a forbidden fruit that she desperately wanted a bite of.

We raced to see who could get naked first. Before she could even get her bra off I strapped on a condom for safe measure and was inside her. She let out a moan of relief like she had missed me for a lifetime. I was just getting started.

She wrapped her legs around me and I picked her up off the bed and carried her to my dresser while still inside her, pressed play on my iPod dock, and reached for a bottle of vodka.

"Want a shot?"

She nodded quickly over and over while her breathing turned to hyperventilation. I took a swig, held it in my mouth, and then fed it to her like a famished baby bird while continuing my upward-thrusting rhythm. Then we dove back into each other's faces tongue first and I began writing the sexual equivalent to Beethoven's final symphony.

I will try to the best of my ability to describe the bombardment of positions that took place.

First: I had her pinned against my dresser with both hands under her knees, bouncing her up and down like she was riding a toy unicorn in a playground.

Second: I had my knees on the edge of my bed with my hands on the floor. She had her legs wrapped around me with the back of her head on the ground as I performed a grown man's pile driver on her.

Third: I was sitting on my desk chair taking pulls of Kentucky Deluxe while she bounced with her back toward me and I sang along to "Sweet Home Alabama."

Fourth: We were on the floor and I had both of her legs over my shoulders with both hands gripping her ass while she yelled pleasure-filled obscenities at me. I took a second to silently thank Kelli for the night she unleashed the beast within.

Fifth: We broke into Turbo's room, who was visiting his out-of-state buddies, and Katherine was taking rips from his water bong while I spanked her ass from behind with Turbo's pledge paddle.

Sixth: We were on the crow's nest of the third floor and she was moaning into the night sky bent over the railing while I smoked a cigarette and rocked her like a wagon wheel. Anyone on Greek Row wondering who was the fucking man now had their answer. That included her boyfriend and all his brothers.

Seventh: Still on the crow's nest, she told me she had come enough times and that it was my turn, and then started blowing me. After a few minutes she stopped, looked up at me, and said, "You can go in my mouth," and on cue I did just that.

I woke up in my bed with my Dave Matthews playlist still playing on my iPod, and a note next to my bed.

Townes,
  That was the best night of my life. I have to see you again soon.

Katherine

She put the imprint of her lipstick next to her name. Mission accomplished. I came into school an unproven rookie, and through years of hard work, dedication, and respect for the game, I gained experience and became a hardened veteran. After more than five years of sport-fucking the finest girls this country has to offer, my future wife will always look at me post-orgasm and wonder how I learned the things I did.

———

Sex and relationships in college are completely different than in any other part of life. The constant presence of parties, alcohol, and a never-ending sea of the opposite sex in your age range make meeting people who are down to fuck incredibly easy...

On Intercourse and Relationships

Switching to doggy style when the SportsCenter *top 10 comes on. TFM.*

Barely doing your part in a 69. TFM.

The "hey beautiful" mass text to every girl in your phone at 2:00 a.m. TFM.

Inviting a girl to come watch a movie, and filming one instead. TFM.

Telling her you're "getting close" during a blowjob when you're nowhere near being done. TFM.

She put out her hand so I would hold it. I gave her a low five. TFM.

My wartime strategies and sexual tendencies coincide. Never pull out. TFM.

Putting a mirror at the end of the hallway so girls have to watch themselves do the walk of shame. TFM.

My girlfriend is in town. What a cock block. TFM.

There are two types of girls in this world: my mom and sluts. TFM.

Taking her out for ice cream. TFM.

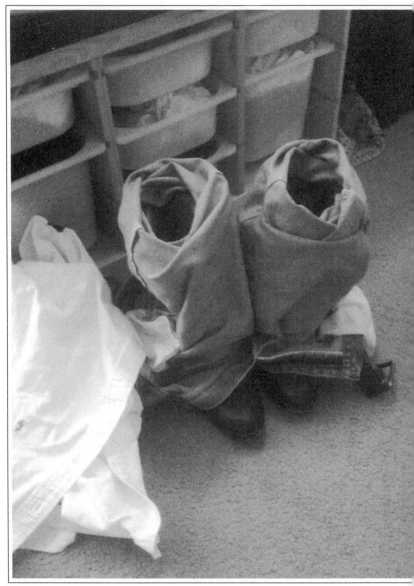

Firefighter-inspired clothing exit. TFM.

Waking up to the smell of two slams cooking breakfast in shacker shirts. TFM.

Giving an approval honk for the walk of shame. TFM.

Doing Time

DEALING WITH THE COPS IS JUST ANOTHER PART OF LIFE when your fraternity orchestrates the mass consumption of alcohol at parties that go far beyond maximum occupancy, violate city noise ordinances, ignore every section of the fire code, and take pride in breaking as many rules as possible on a regular basis. Of course I'm not talking about a sophisticated team of highly trained super police, but occasionally University PD stops playing Angry Birds on their phones and handing out MIPs long enough to actually arrest someone. Regardless of jurisdiction, when a cop slaps the cuffs on one of my pledge brothers or me, it always makes for an entertaining story, three of which are legendary and need to be shared with the world. They have been recounted by what I saw personally, what the arrested remember, and resulting police reports.

Stadium Mayhem

It was homecoming my sophomore year and I was twenty-two rows up in the student section of our stadium. Every fraternity and sorority sat in the same block and we were notorious for being incredibly fucking rowdy. Hundreds of girls in game-day dresses intermingled with guys in button-downs, khakis, boots, and boat shoes. I was in the heart of it with four of the ten whiskey Pocket Shots I had snuck into the stadium still stuffed into my jeans and boots. (Pocket Shots are small plastic bags filled with liquor, sold at gas stations, and made for the sole purpose of sneaking into events.) The rest were resting in the comfort of my stomach with a dozen tailgate beers and a couple morning mimosas.

The air was filled with the strong smell of hot dogs and pop-corn from the stadium concessions, and smoke from the grills at tailgate clung to everyone's clothing. With every snap of the football the crowd grew more belligerent, hurling obscenities at the opposing team and starting insult-filled chants aimed at their cheerleaders.

Our first visit from the police came in the second quarter when Turbo decided to rip a one-hitter in his seat. He sat down and took a hit of weed, using the standing crowd as cover so stadium security wouldn't spot him, but the smoke and reaction from everyone around him gave away his general position. When he saw the smoke, our section's security guard pulled a walkie-talkie from his orange vest and used it to call for backup. A real police officer shaped like a bowling ball waddled out of the tunnel and panted heavily on his way up the steep steps to see what the problem was. After a short conversation with security he yelled out over our area.

"Who's smoking? Put out that cigarette!" Apparently he didn't have a nose for marijuana, which could explain his sta-dium detail. "You know there's no smoking in here!"

I cupped my hands over my mouth and booed loudly along with the other Alphas in my row. The cop shuffled up and down the aisle ducking and trying to get his eyes on the rule breaker, but Turbo had already pocketed the pipe and was casually clapping with everyone else.

"Don't make me come back here," warned the cop as he waddled back down the rafters.

By halftime we were up 28–0 and celebrating accordingly. Three additional stadium security personnel from sections filled with rule-abiding GDIs had come over to make sure things in our section didn't boil over. Guys who snuck in flasks were being extra careful not to be spotted as they mixed their drinks. I was in between whiskey-Cokes, waiting for Monte to get back from his turn at the concession stand with more mixers.

A girl named Brooke I had met at a couple of parties was sitting in front of me drinking vodka-lemonade all game, turning around and flirting every time our team did something good. The first time we scored she turned around and high-fived me, the second time she hugged my waist, and the third time she playfully patted my crotch like my dick was responsible for the touchdown. I was trying to get her to commit to coming to the Alpha house later that night when Monte returned with my drink. I checked to make sure I wasn't being watched by security before pulling one of the shots from my boot and tearing away the top of the plastic, but before I could dump it into my drink, Brooke grabbed my hand.

"This is my last homecoming, you know," she said. "It like totally sucks."

"Well, you should make sure it's the best one," I responded.

"Well, you should take that shot in a way we'll both remember." She tilted her head back and opened her mouth.

"You know this is whiskey?" I asked.

She nodded innocently. I glanced up and down the aisle

and dumped the shot into her mouth. She pulled me down, tilted my head, and kissed me, letting the liquor run in with her tongue.

"Mid-game makeout!" Monte announced to the crowd.

"Get in there, Townes!" someone chimed in.

I swallowed the whiskey and she pulled away from me laughing.

"Well, that's my new favorite way to drink," I said.

She motioned for me to lean in and whispered in my ear, "I've got a better way."

"Well, maybe you can show me tonight at the house," I played back.

Her luscious lips curled upward as she smiled at me. "Or maybe...I could show you right now."

Without hesitation I pulled another shot from my boot and handed it to her. She put her knees up on the bleachers and dropped one dress strap from her shoulder.

"Off my tits."

I lost the small amount of focus I still had on the football game. She dropped the other strap and pulled her sundress down just enough so I could get my face in between her big tits while she dumped whiskey down her cleavage waterslide into my mouth. Judging from her form I was pretty sure she had done this before. For a second I wondered if the judgment from other girls and possible attention from security made this worthwhile, but then a chant broke out.

"Townes! Townes! Townes! Townes!"

"Let's give the people what they want," I told Brooke.

I was kneeling down and positioning my chin for maximum motorboat efficiency when an unwelcome voice caught my ears.

"Don't you fucking do it!"

The stadium security guard in the orange vest was standing at the end of my row, pointing at me while fans booed him and rained empty cups down in his direction. I kept my head between her tits and looked up to see if she had noticed him. She looked down at me and said, "You're not going to let *him* ruin this, are you?"

"You! In the white visor!" the security guard continued.

He gauged my nonreaction and started to make his way down the aisle. I looked him dead in the eye, pressed two handfuls of Brooke's tits to my cheeks, and opened my mouth. She dumped the shot down her chest and I slurped it up with my tongue as fast as I could, sucking on her skin.

The security guard yelled in a frustrated rage and barreled through the row of fans, who were chanting my name. Thankfully my loyal supporters didn't make it easy for him, and I had time to take off down the aisle in the opposite direction.

I vaulted down the steps while the crowd cheered me on, looking back to check the rent-a-cop's progress. He broke out of the crowd and quickly chopped his steps down the stairs with his walkie-talkie in hand. I could feel every eye of the student section on me, and I turned toward them and raised both hands valiantly over my head. The crowd exploded.

At the bottom of the stairs I turned to the concession area to make my escape, but the chunky waddling cop was headed up the ramp toward me. Another cop came running out of the ramp behind me.

"That's enough! Stop!" someone yelled.

Adrenaline took over and I hurdled the railing onto the barricade between the bleachers and the field, which was absolutely forbidden. I struggled to keep my balance, running along the foot-wide concrete wall while the alcohol sloshed around in my stomach. I saw several orange vests pushing through the crowd toward me, but looking back over my shoulder I saw no sign of my original pursuer.

Then I caught a glimpse of an orange blur in my peripheral vision. It was him. He must have cut through another section to head me off. From a full sprint he left his feet and gave a Hulk-like roar as he soared through the air. I tried to dodge him, but he clipped my shoulder and we both tumbled eight feet down onto the field. I landed hard on my back, knocking the air out of me, and let out a groan of pain. The lunatic rolled over and climbed on top of me, pinning both of my arms to the ground under his knees.

"There!" he yelled. "Who's the badass now? Huh? Who's the big man now?"

He had gone totally berserk, slamming his fists into the grass as the veins in his neck bulged out and his eyes widened with rage. I struggled to get my arms out from under him as he reared back his right hand and let out a high-pitched scream.

"BYAHHHHH!"

But just as he was about to swing, two cops tore him away from me.

One of the officers stood me up and pulled my hands behind my back, applying a zip-tie to my wrists. The entire student section was in a frenzy as the game became secondary entertainment to my arrest. Two officers took my arms and another walked in front, leading me through the tunnel into the stadium's facilities. Two others escorted the fuming security guard behind me.

"Fucking frat boy!" he yelled as they pulled him into a separate holding room.

That put a smile on my face, much to the displeasure of one officer. He patted me down, took my wallet from my back pocket, and slammed me down onto a bench by my shoulders.

"You want me to tell you how we're going to handle this, Mr. Prescott?" he asked, tapping my ID with his finger.

"Yes sir." I nodded.

"We're going to take you out of the stadium, and you're gonna go home and be thankful that moron snapped on you, because otherwise you'd be under arrest."

"That sounds good, sir," I responded. "I wouldn't want to have to press charges."

He yanked my hands up behind my back to cut the zip-tie loose.

"Don't push it. And if I ever have a problem with you again I can promise you won't see the inside of this stadium until you graduate."

In the end I got off with nothing but a couple of bruised ribs. I probably could've sued the crazed security guard, but it wouldn't have been worth it, especially considering that the entire ordeal made me a legend. I got celebrity treatment at tailgates, a journalism student wanted to interview me as part of a piece he was doing on drinking and football, and yes, I took Brooke down that night.

The Wild West Joy Ride

The spring of our sophomore year Turbo was invited to a Kappa date party by a girl named Jennifer. She was way out of his fucking league, and we reminded him of that on a semi-hourly basis. She was tan with long, toned legs, a good face, a flat stomach, and a great pair of bikini bombs. Once when I was shooting hoops at the rec I saw her dominating the Stairmaster with enough force to power a small city. Turbo was an average ass clown who hadn't set foot inside a weight room since high school lacrosse, with drug habits that would impress Lindsay Lohan. How did he get her to invite him? He took too much Molly and they had an emotional heart-to-heart about religion on the crow's nest during an "Anything but Clothes" theme party, which resulted in her thinking he was some super-sensitive guy. The next day he got a text asking if he'd go with her to Kappa's Wild West Date Dash.

After their last function, Jennifer's chapter had gotten into some hot water with their national office when several girls spewed puke all over a charter bus, and as part of their punishment they were no longer allowed to rent buses. As fate would have it, Jennifer's Suburban had to have some work done over Christmas break, so she drove one of her dad's cars, a renovated red 1967 Mustang, back to campus for the spring semester. So Jennifer, Turbo, Jennifer's best friend Allie, and Allie's date Jeff all packed into her dad's favorite classic car and headed thirty minutes down the highway to a dance hall in the hill country where the Wild West Date Dash was being held.

I was at the party rocking cowboy boots, Wranglers, and a pearl snap button-down with a Kappa named Sarah who was their vice president at the time, which unfortunately meant I couldn't get completely wasted. On the plus side, I got to witness and remember all of Turbo's antics, which together with his testament helped me document this story.

At 10:15 p.m. he staggered in forty-five minutes late with his date under his arm. He was wearing a giant foam cowboy hat, denim vest with no shirt, jean shorts cut off mid-thigh, and boots. Around his waist he had two fake six-shooters holstered to his belt. Jennifer looked like a high-dollar Native American prostitute in a tan fabric one-piece costume that was frayed at the bottom and barely covering any of her irresistible legs. She was also rocking a headband with two colorful feathers and two stripes of red war paint under each eye. If she had been a real Indian there would've been nonstop bloodshed between tribes over her ass.

They entered the mob of denim and leather, and Turbo's ridiculous outfit got some laughs as he carelessly walked through the crowd to the bar. From both of their staggering walks I could tell they had taken part in a solid pregame. He grabbed two Cokes and headed to the bathroom, obviously to empty one of his flasks into them. A few of the older Kappas eyed him and shook their heads in disapproval. Jennifer pretended not to notice, beaming with joy knowing she had the craziest date at the party, and when he reemerged they twisted their way into the middle of the dance floor.

In no time the two of them were noticeably the most shit-faced couple at the event. They fumbled around the dance floor while Turbo yelled "Yeehaw!" over and over and fired one of his fake pistols into the air. Jennifer posed with a group of ten girls for a picture, but just before the flash Turbo leapt in front of them and pointed both guns at the camera.

"Turbo, stooooop," said Jennifer, smiling. The other girls were not pleased.

Around 10:30, after repeatedly falling down while attempting to two-step to Brooks & Dunn's "Boot Scootin' Boogie," they started making out in the middle of the dance floor while Turbo cupped her ass with both hands. I noticed a couple of other guys eyeing Jennifer's backside as Turbo gave it a squeeze, and one of them got caught by his date, who hit him with her rubber tomahawk. Sororities have designated "Standards" committees that reprimand girls for what they deem "unbecoming behavior," and at that point my date Sarah informed me that Jennifer had a 100 percent chance of being called to Standards. Turbo had completely corrupted her.

By 11:30 everyone under twenty-one who didn't sneak in booze or have a fake ID was starting to sober up, while Turbo was making yet another mixed drink in the middle of the dance floor with the backup flask from his boot. When he offered Jennifer a drink she said, "I should probably just have a few sips of yours, babe," so he offered Allie's date, Jeff, some of his whiskey. When Jeff didn't immediately offer some to Allie they got into a dramatic argument that resulted in Allie taking his drink, chugging it, and Jeff stomping off in anger. Not only had Turbo managed to get his own date completely sloshed, now he had her best friend acting like a lush and fighting with her date.

These sorority functions were always over by midnight (to keep the girls from drinking too much), which just left more time for after-parties on Greek Row. At 11:45 p.m., fifteen minutes before the end of the Date Dash, Turbo stumbled up to the bar where I was talking with Sarah and steadied himself with a hand on my shoulder.

"Hey, we're going to bounce out of here early so we can swing by the gas station on the way to the house before they stop selling beer."

"You should probably get Jeff to drive," I said.

"Allie has no fucking idea where that loser went. I'm driving the 'stang. Are you gonna throw in for beer or not?"

"Tim, don't be stupid," said Sarah. "You can ride back with us after I get everyone out of here. We can get her car tomorrow, and I'm sure y'all have beer at the house."

Turbo took a sip of his whiskey drink and glared at her.

"What if there's not, Sarah? Then what? I'm going."

With that he turned around, grabbing Jennifer and Allie.

"I can't wait to get behind the wheel of this speed demon," he said.

"You're okay to drive, though, right?" asked Jennifer.

"Oh yeah, absolutely." Then he put his arm around each girl and headed out into the parking lot.

I considered telling Sarah I wasn't feeling well and joining him in what seemed like a guaranteed lay situation, but my conscience kept me in line.

Turbo helped Allie into the back and held the door while Jennifer kissed him on the cheek and wearily plopped down into the passenger seat. Allie immediately took the Malibu rum they'd been pregaming with out from under the backseat and took a pull while Turbo peeled out of the parking lot. Down the dirt road, before the highway, he pulled into a Phillips 66 and grabbed two cases of Natty Light. By the time he got back in the car Jennifer was passed out cold and Allie was clutching the rum, nodding her head along with the radio.

He shook his head and threw the beer in the back with Allie, who immediately opened the case, cracked a beer, and handed it to him. He pulled onto the highway and immediately gunned it up to 85 mph, completely ignoring the speed limit because he'd never had control of anything with that much horsepower. It was late, so there weren't many cars on the road, and it was a straight shot back to campus. Jennifer started snoring in the seat next to him, and Turbo switched gears and punched the gas up to 95 mph, smiling happily with a gorgeous girl passed out in the passenger seat, flying down an empty road with a cold beer in his hand. That's when Allie leaned over and whispered in his ear.

"God, the way you drive this car is sexy."

She reached over into the front seat, turned up the music, and unzipped his jeans. Turbo glanced over at Jennifer, who was still in a deep sleep, and tried to stay in his lane while Allie started giving him a handjob like a hippie hitchhiker.

"The faster you go, the faster I go," she said.

He grinned. "I can play that game."

He punched the gas and got up to 110 mph while she pumped furiously and the engine roared. He lost focus momentarily while Allie worked his human stickshift and had to swerve around a minivan, which caused Jennifer to slump over in her seat. Allie sat back quickly and Turbo took off his hat and put it over his boner. Jennifer didn't wake, though, and Allie went straight back to her handiwork.

"Faster," she whispered.

He gunned it again and got up to 120 mph. He was flying down the highway like a bat out of hell, so distracted by the fact that he was getting a pump-job from his date's best friend that he almost missed the exit for campus. He switched four lanes at once and skidded into the exit lane while applying the brakes to slow down. Allie licked his earlobe slowly, and the simultaneous effects of her gripping his dick, the engine vibrating his balls, and the adrenaline from a high-speed race against no one culminated in one gigantic cum shot all over the steering wheel. Allie giggled and kissed him on the cheek.

"Looks like I win," she said. "In record time."

Then she sat back in her seat while he tucked his dick back into his jeans and looked for something to wipe down the steering wheel while he turned onto University Drive. He couldn't find anything, so at the next stop sign he used the corner of his vest to smear his man load from the wheel. That's when he checked the rearview and saw the cop behind him.

"Fucking shit," he said.

"What is it?" asked Allie as she looked back through the window. "Oh shit."

The squad car's lights weren't on, but as Turbo pulled up to the Kappa house and into a parking spot the cop pulled in horizontally behind him and threw on the flashers.

Turbo started to panic and rolled the half-empty beer from his cup holder under the passenger seat.

"Shut off the engine and put both hands on the steering wheel," the officer said through the siren speaker.

Turbo put his hands on the steering wheel and Allie started to freak out.

"What the hell did you do? Did you run a stop sign? I've got a bottle back here!"

"Hide it, fast," Turbo said, trying not to move his lips as the officer exited his car.

Allie's panic woke Jennifer, who immediately saw the flashing red and blue lights in her side mirror and started hyperventilating in a full-blown panic attack. The officer approached the car and Turbo rolled down the window.

"License and registration, son."

Turbo handed him his license. "This isn't my car."

"Whose car is it?"

"Her dad's." He nodded to Jennifer.

The officer pointed at the steering wheel.

"What's that liquid?"

"That's nothing, sir," Turbo responded.

"Well, we got several reports of a vehicle matching this

description driving *dangerously* at a high rate of speed on the highway. Have you been drinking?"

"I had one beer," Turbo admitted.

"Why in the hell are you all dressed like that?"

"We were at a sorority event."

"Step out of the car, son."

Turbo got out of the car and tried to stand as straight as possible in front of the officer, who extended his thumb six inches from Turbo's face.

"Mr. Rumsen, I need you to stop swaying and blow on my thumb."

"Blow on your thumb? What the—I mean...sir...what?"

"Just blow on my thumb, son."

He blew and the officer leaned in to smell his breath.

"One beer, huh? That has got to be the strongest goddamn beer ever brewed. I'm going to have you perform a series of tests to determine how much you've had to drink. Do you comply?"

He took a second to think about it.

"Respectfully, sir, I want my lawyer and I'm not doing anything until I see him."

"Then let's take a walk over to my car."

"Shotgun!" Turbo chimed in.

"Oh, you want to be a smartass?" the officer snapped.

He slammed him into the side of the car and handcuffed him. Turbo got popped with an MIP and charged with DWI. He refused the breathalyzer at the station and his lawyer eventually got the DWI charge dropped down to reckless driving after shaping the story to make it seem like Turbo was just trying to get two incredibly drunk girls home safely, which was partially true. Allie and Jennifer were both given MIPs and put on probation by Kappa. It became a tradition for ballsy Alphas to call "Shotgun!" when being escorted to police cars to carry on Turbo's tradition.

Naked Nate Is Drugged

Our senior year we headed to Gulf Shores, Alabama, for Spring Break, where we had rented a beach house that slept sixteen, eight Alphas and eight girls. Nate was the only one of us who wasn't twenty-one, but he had a flawless fake ID that he had been using since we were pledges. It scanned, had all the right shit show up under a black light, and had never been turned down. Alabama police were notoriously hardcore about busting fake IDs during Spring Break, but Nate wasn't worried.

"This thing is unstoppable," he said. "I could use it to board a fucking airplane as Mr. Paul Allen."

Most of the girls staying in our house were smokeshows, and a few were even dating material, but one was a latch-on that we just couldn't shake. All around she was the creepiest and most annoying girl I had ever met. She weighed at least 180, and that's probably the nicest thing I can say about her. One time I woke up in the frat castle and she was sitting at my desk slurping an iced coffee and watching me sleep. It was terrifying, and to this day I sleep with my bedroom door locked. Regrettably, sometimes girls come in package deals where you have to accept an extremely sore thumb in order to hang with her hot friends. Our sore thumb's name was Morgan, and unfortunately for Nate she had recently become obsessed with him. All Nate's friends, myself included, had assured Morgan that Nate was interested in order to further complicate the situation for him.

The first night of the trip Morgan was gunning hard for Nate. The drunker she got the more painfully and awkwardly obvious it became. During a game of flip cup on the beach house balcony she walked up behind him, wrapped her arms around his waist, pressed her face to his back, and just stood there for a few minutes while he went on playing. It temporarily weakened the collective morale of our group. Regardless, Nate managed to fend her off. Around 3:30 a.m. when we were all drinking on the patio he oddly announced that he was going to take a piss, locked himself in the room he was supposed to be sharing with me, and passed out. That led to Morgan repeatedly asking me, "Are you sure he's okay in there? Maybe we should kick the door in." For a while I considered it, but decided to pass out on the couch like a good friend.

On the second night we all went out to the bar a few blocks away and Nate took 40 milligrams of Adderall to make sure he could stay out drinking longer than Morgan. After the bar closed we headed to another beach house that some younger Alphas had rented and combined forces for a giant beach party. Morgan valiantly tried to keep up with Nate until 4 a.m. before she conceded and headed back to our house to crash. Nate didn't come home until 5:30 a.m., just to be safe and make sure she was asleep. But on the third day of the trip, after two nights of gentle rejection, Morgan was fed up and decided to take matters into her own disturbingly large hands.

We all went out to dinner, and that's when things started to get weird. Morgan practically stiff-armed her way through the other girls to get a seat next to Nate, which was pretty standard behavior for her. But later, when we were waiting on dessert, Rogers spilled his drink on himself and all of us started laughing. It was funny for a few seconds…but Nate didn't stop. He cackled uncontrollably and obnoxiously slapped his hands on the table, knocking silverware everywhere. After a few minutes a waiter came over and asked if he could please wait outside until we had paid our bill. I walked him out and told him to smoke a cigarette to calm down.

"What the fuck is wrong with you?" I asked. "Did you hit the goddamn vaporizer with Turbo?"

He couldn't even talk, just shook his head and kept snickering like a fucking idiot while he pulled on his cigarette. I figured he must have eaten a weed brownie or something, so I just kept drinking and expected that time would cure his delusional behavior. It didn't.

An hour later we were at Flora-Bama in Perdido Key (on the Alabama/Florida border, about fifteen miles from our beach house) when I looked down the bar and saw Nate with his shirt off, waving it over his head while he wiggled out of his pants and Morgan cheered him on. A bouncer was trying to pull his shirt back down over his head when I ran over to help keep him from stripping down.

"Woah, woah, Nate, keep your fucking pants on!"

"This is no-man's-land!" he yelled toward the ceiling with his arms stretched overhead as the bouncer re-dressed him.

Nate had officially transformed into Naked Nate, also known as The Nude. I had seen him do this plenty of times, but considering the circumstances it was less funny and more annoying than usual. I had to slide the bouncer a $20 bill and insist that he'd behave before he let Naked Nate stay inside the bar. I got him to put his fucking shirt back on and then pulled him back toward our table. I didn't let go of his arm until I was ready to take a seat, because I knew he would undress again the first chance he got, but when I reached for my drink the slippery fuck made a break for the door.

"That's it," I said. "Your turn, Turbo. You gave him the drugs, you babysit him."

"I didn't give him shit," he said. "Nothing I take makes you into a fucking nudist, but fine. I'll grab him."

"Maybe I should come," Morgan offered with a creepily exaggerated smile on her face.

"Don't worry about it," said Turbo. "I'm just going to get him in a cab back to the house."

He took off through the crowd and I went back to drinking and hitting on some Zetas from Florida. Fifteen minutes later Morgan stumbled up to me on the dance floor with tears in her eyes.

"What the hell happened?" I asked.

"I might've done something bad," she said, swaying and biting her nails.

"What'd you do?"

"I just wanted him to like me! I just wanted him to relax!"

I grabbed her by the shoulders and shook. "What the fuck did you do?"

"Just two Ambien! That's all! I put them in his beer."

"Oh fuck."

Turbo ran up to us and said he couldn't find Nate anywhere. We ran back outside together, but he was nowhere to be found. We drove around the surrounding streets for a half hour before heading back to our house to see if maybe he got a cab home, but he wasn't there either.

After calling the jails and every hotel, I sacked up and called the hospitals on both sides of the border. To our relief, it turned out Nate was indeed checked in with a broken ankle, but at the hospital across the state line in Florida. I asked when we could pick him up, but the nurse said he would be booked in at the county jail in the morning because he had been arrested for public intoxication and evading arrest before being brought to the emergency room.

Nate didn't remember a single fucking thing when the police woke him up in the hospital bed at 5 a.m. the next morning, but when the officer called him "Paul" and he checked his hospital wristband and saw "Paul Allen," he realized something had gone terribly wrong. He had Band-Aids on his arm from where they drew blood, and a cast on his left foot where he fractured his ankle. Once his lawyers got their hands on the police report he emailed it out to our entire chapter.

Officer Jim Young's Narrative

(Mr. Nathan Johnson is referred to as "Mr. Allen" due to false government documentation)

March 16 1322

Officer Jacobs and I were dispatched to the Waffle House at 17352 Perdido Key to investigate a disturbing the peace complaint that was called in by a Ms. [Redacted].

Upon approach we saw Mr. Paul Allen climbing a palm tree shirtless, at which time I shined my vehicle's spotlight on his back and told him to come down immediately. Mr. Allen did not comply and continued to climb, so I stepped out of my vehicle and approached the tree. When I shined my flashlight at the base of the tree and again told Mr. Allen to descend using my light as a guide, he removed his pants along with his underwear and threw them down at me before shouting an expletive, leaping from the tree and running down the 600 block.

Ofc Jacobs took out his taser and fired at Mr. Allen, missing short as he ran. Ofc Jacobs then pursued the suspect on foot and I reentered my vehicle and followed Ofc Jacobs in pursuit of Mr. Allen across the street. The suspect was nearly hit by traffic on his way into a bank parking lot.

Ofc Jacobs caught up to Mr. Allen and brought him down by the waist, pinning his legs beneath Ofc Jacobs's torso during the fall.

Mr. Allen continued to resist Ofc Jacobs by yelling "rape" repeatedly and trying to wiggle free. At this point I exited my vehicle and applied my handcuffs to the suspect. His ankle was badly twisted when he was tackled so I radioed for an ambo. After wrapping his nude body in a towel and talking with Mr. Allen I noted a strong odor of an alcoholic beverage coming from his breath and/or person. He was badly slurring his words and having trouble keeping his eyes open.

Mr. Allen was then notified he was being charged with Public Intoxication and Evading Arrest, but would first be taken to the emergency room to be treated for his injury . . .

In the end Nate decided not to press charges against Morgan after his charges were dropped when his lawyer convinced the judge that he was randomly drugged at a bar, citing his blood work as evidence.

When I asked him if he'd rather take a PI and resisting arrest charge or let Morgan ride him like a horse he said, "I would rather fuck a pine cone every night for the rest of my life."

When living a lifestyle that pretty much depends upon breaking the rules, legal issues are bound to come up. This leads to hilarious encounters with the police, a misplaced sense of pride in being arrested, and the overall feeling that the fraternity is above the law...

On Breaking the Law

Doing something you shouldn't just because everyone is chanting your name. TFM.

Calling shotgun when being escorted to a cop car. TFM.

Waking up in the hospital with your fake ID's name on your wristband. TFM.

Asking your arresting officer if you can hang your blazer in the front seat. TFM.

Being known as "the drunk guy" in the drunk tank. TFM.

Getting pulled over and letting the cop off with a warning. TFM.

Leaving out the words "court mandated" when telling your mom about your community service hours. TFM.

Asking campus police when the real cops are going to show up. TFM.

Carpooling to your court date with the judge. TFM.

Being mistaken for one of the lawyers in court. TFM.

Adding the final exam for court ordered DUI school to the fraternity test bank. TFM.

When you're with people that matter, the illegal things you do don't. TFM.

The great lawyers of tomorrow breaking an absurd number of laws today. TFM.

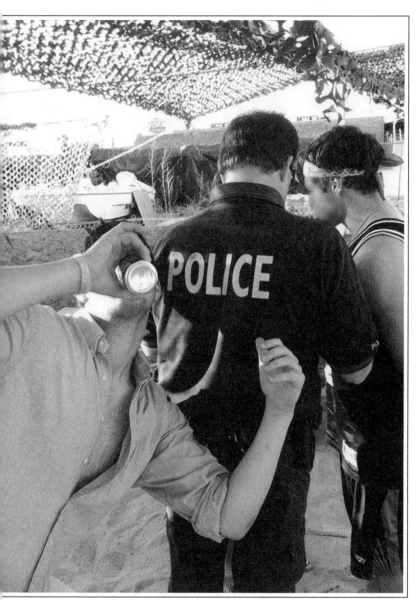

Behind the back of the law. TFM.

Drunk drive-thru. TFM.

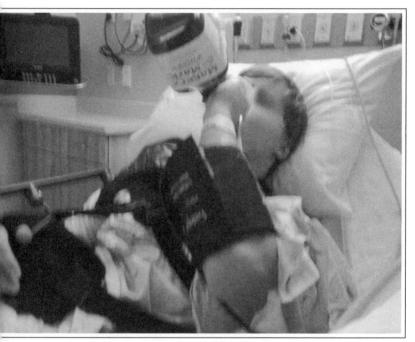

Supplying your own painkiller. TFM.

Road Trip Raging

PEOPLE ALWAYS TALK ABOUT COLLEGE LIKE THERE'S NO opportunity to elongate the experience. I was always told, "Townes, college will be the best four years of your life," but the truth is that anyone who graduates from college on time is a moron. I have a cousin who graduated magna cum laude from Vanderbilt in three years. She probably had sober sex, snuck around her dorm's musty hallways a few times— giggling past curfew—and made dean's list all six pathetically short semesters spent almost entirely in the library. Congratulations? Every Easter, Thanksgiving, and Christmas I remind her she's a GDI failure in my eyes. As you know by now, I made sure to take full advantage of every second I earned on campus, leaving a trail of destruction in my wake.

Each memory I've shared with you is precious to me, but none more than Alpha's formal during my first senior year. Even if you decide five, six, or eight years of undergraduate studies are necessary to absorb a suitable dosage of the college experience, you still only get four spring formals (assuming you pledge your first semester like a fucking man). For the third consecutive year we voted New Orleans as our destination, so we were all familiar with the morally corrupt city with which we were dealing. The mind has to be in a disturbed place to handle the shit that occurs in that town, and normal livers can't handle the amount of alcohol we forced ours to absorb during our stay. So I spent weeks preparing myself mentally (by skipping class) and physically (by drinking, fucking, hazing, and playing golf as often as possible).

When it comes to formal, the bus ride ends up being almost half the fun. The nine-hour pilgrimage is nearly as dangerous as Bourbon Street itself, and the seniors' bus is indisputably the most volatile, because for us (the old balls) this is the last hurrah, and we just don't give a fuck. During this final voyage the goal is to shatter any remnants of your moral compass and come out of the three-day fog with as many inappropriate stories as possible. All the while it's important to keep your date's level of respect for you, or her BAC, high enough that she'll still let you drunkenly pound her privates. Otherwise, you'll end up trolling the hallways of the hotel for randoms, or worse.

Our caravan of charter buses planned to leave at 8 a.m. on Friday to ensure a suitable arrival time in the Big Easy. Some people had Friday class, but showing up wasn't even an option. Weeks ahead of time, Nate and I arranged to take two freshman girls from different sororities as our dates. We figured their unfamiliarity with each other would give them an opportunity to discuss *The Bachelorette* and how much they adore Diet Coke. Apparently I had met my date, and invited her to formal, at a bar on a Tuesday night the week before. None of which I remembered. The following day I received a text from a contact I had saved as "9":

3:13 p.m.: *OMG totes excited about New Orleans! It's gonna be the best weekend ever k call me soon Townes!!!!!!!!!*

It took me an hour or so to figure out who she was, but when I did, I wasn't disappointed. Her name was Katie Groom, and yes, she was stacked. The number 9 must've been my drunken assessment of her good looks. We picked up Katie from the Omega house and Nate's date from Kappa, and then made our way to the frat castle. It was early and I was battling a hangover, so it wasn't until boarding the bus that I realized these two rookie slams were both wearing sundresses appropriate for a day at the racetrack. They were completely oblivious to the level of filthiness about to take place during the drive.

The drinking started immediately. Coolers were packed in the far back of the bus and spread throughout the aisles. Katie had stuffed mine with a case of Keystone, a bottle of Woodford Reserve, and a box of wine for herself. The backpacks stored in the overhead compartments were crammed full of tobacco products, snacks, and miscellaneous drugs. The instant the driver fired up the diesel engine, Turbo downed a beer bong filled with whiskey. By 10 a.m. he'd be an unstoppable force of destruction, full-sprinting in the opposite direction of the finish line that should've been his date's vagina. As we pulled out of the parking lot the movie *Top Gun* began on the TV screens, and Monte started a roaring "USA! USA! USA!" chant, inaugurating the trip. Some sorostitutes who thought they'd be able to get some sleep were caught off guard by the swift start of binge drinking and obnoxious patriotic noise-making. They reluctantly joined in to avoid standing out like heteros at a gay pride parade.

One of the more entertaining aspects of the trip was observing the interactions of sorority girls suddenly thrown into a frenzied situation together. The spirit of camaraderie between brothers was at an all-time high. Testosterone was flowing as high fives were exchanged, and beers were being shotgunned on every aisle. Contrarily, the awkward disdain that the grab bag of random dates pretend not to have for each other was also at an all-time high. Miraculously, two girls who normally wouldn't acknowledge one another's existence conversed when forced to sit a few feet from each other. I'm no zoologist, but I'm pretty sure this is what it's like when two lesbian pandas scissor each other after being caged in captivity for an extended period of time. The tension was eased with the nonstop flow of Franzia box wine, and slowly these girls found they might not be so different after all; some just prefer Lilly Pulitzer to Vera Bradley. Regardless, they had no choice but to become allies if they wished to survive the days ahead, both socially and physically. What else were they going to do? Their dates were too busy drunkenly reminiscing on pledgeship and form-tackling each other.

Two hours in, someone toward the front of the bus broke out weed brownies and Adderall, then passed them around to the casual drug users surrounding him. Not only was everyone already buzzed on whatever booze they'd decided to start the morning with, but thirty minutes later several passengers were so high that they struggled to sit still, wide-eyed and grinding their teeth. As I polished off my seventh beer, I asked Katie if she wanted either of the aforementioned substances. She quickly shook her head as she looked at me like a terrified puppy during a violent thunderstorm.

"No! I mean...no thanks. I'm good with my wine!"

"That's fine. Just being a gentleman," I responded as I put my arm around her and gave a reassuring everything-is-going-to-be-okay squeeze.

I don't know how much we paid the Greyhound bus drivers,

because I wasn't the fucking treasurer, but it wasn't enough. It seems to me that hauling our hedonistic asses to NOLA would be far more entertaining than driving a bus full of near-death stiffs to an Indian casino, but for whatever reason they didn't appreciate having beer funneled onto their heads while they drove down the interstate in the early morning. The poor guy had already gotten on the loudspeaker twice and respectfully asked that we "calm down a bit." We responded to his request with a chorus of boos, and Turbo shouted, "DO YOUR FUCKING JOB, PEASANT!"

By noon, things really started to get out of hand. The line for the bathroom on the bus was unacceptable, so Nate made his date into a human curtain so he could piss into a bottle already half filled with dip spit. Everyone was entirely too fucked up, and the drivers pulled over in the middle of nowhere to gas up and give people a chance to grab some fresh air. This was every gas station's bad wet dream: three buses of drunken lunatics descending onto their property, knocking over aisles of chips and gum and blowing hundreds of dollars on pork rinds and sexual lubricant. They had a rack of American flag bandanas. It was gone. They had fifty packs of Marlboro Lights. They vanished. A few of the couples didn't exit the bus, but awkwardly remained under blankets trying to play off the fact that they were participating in dry hand-jobbing and finger blasting. Everyone else chain-smoked cigarettes outside, and raided the gas station for munchies, more nicotine, and more alcohol. I stumbled through the store and into the restroom, where I found Turbo blowing chunks all over the wall, laughing hysterically as Monte laughed in the stall next to him.

"Turbo, uh... you all right there, chief?"

"Yeah, I'm fine. Why do you ask? BLAHHH [projectile vomit]."

"Well, you're spewing all over the wall. Aim at the fucking toilet, psycho. I'll see you back on board."

Once everyone was corralled onto their respective buses, the browbeaten driver attempted to do a head count. He gave up, mumbled something under his breath, and stepped on the gas. Back on the road, five hours in, the chaos continued. Most of the guys had drowned themselves and their dates in enough alcohol to initiate sloppy midday makeouts, clumsily fondling each other. Parsells and Rogers were crushing up Adderall and snorting it to stay awake.

Monte and his perpetual girlfriend Sarah were in one of their good phases, so he'd invited her along and had her straddling him in the back row with a blanket wrapped around them. I'm 99 percent certain there was some shameless public penetration going on. As he smiled and gave a double thumbs-up behind her back, I took a picture with Katie's camera, hoping it would be posted on Facebook for at least a couple hours before it got taken down. Others were slowly coming in and out of consciousness as we rolled toward the Sin City of the South.

———

Pack twenty-five guys with hot dates onto a charter bus filled with as much alcohol as it can hold, tell them they're about to have the time of their lives getting blackout drunk in another city, and then crank up the tunes and let the good times roll. That's the vibe on one of these buses, and it makes for some damn good TFMs...

On Road Trips

The only time you'll find me on a bus is on the way to formal. TFM.

Making charter bus drivers wish they'd chosen a different profession. TFM.

Pissing out the bus window at 70 mph. TFM.

Talking shit to the driver because he hit a pothole during your kegstand. TFM.

Using your blazer as a blanket to turn an OTPHJ into a good old fashioned on the bus. TFM.

The collective "aahhh" at the charter bus piss stop. TFM.

Never getting back the security deposit for the bus. TFM.

On a road trip, we don't "visit" places. We pillage and destroy. We're basically just really well dressed Vikings. TFM.

Luggage. TFM.

Being discreet. TFM.

Almost getting hit doing a Louisville Chugger in the middle of the street. TFM.

Bourbon Street Brutality

BEFORE LONG, OUR LAWLESS CARAVAN WAS IN FRONT of the hotel at the corner of Bourbon and Canal. Someone at the front of the bus turned "Summer of '69" on full blast. It was a bittersweet awakening for those who were passed out. The driver insisted that on our way off we tidy up in order to get back our deposit. We didn't give two shits about the deposit. Everyone booed him again, inaccurately throwing empty cans in his general direction.

Katie and I were in the back of the bus, so I still had time to pound one last beer before exiting. I was too excited to pop the top, and instead performed a Teen Wolf, biting into the side like a fucking animal and spewing it all over myself. Katie looked at me like I was crazy, but I was too drunk to care. As everyone found their way toward the exit, our chapter president tipped the driver $500 for putting up with our shit, and to ensure he gave us a ride home.

I was rooming with Nate, so we met in the lobby for a drink with the girls before heading to our rooms. We wanted to make sure these naïve eighteen-year-olds got properly acquainted so we could attempt a switcheroo, or a four-person

Eiffel Tower. At the very least they needed to feel comfortable being smashed like piñatas in beds just a few feet apart.

While the girls got ready to go out for the night, Nate and I headed to Turbo's room and railed a few lines to get in the zone. We threw on khakis, button-downs, and blazers while Nate attempted to communicate the erratic thoughts firing through his brain at 9,000 rpms.

"It's incredible that in an era of such economic hypocrisy a place like this still exists where men such as ourselves can defy modern moral measures," rattled Nate.

Things can get pretty fucking weird when drugs influence Nate's already overactive mind. I've crafted a standard response to calm him down in these situations.

"I blame the liberals," I replied.

"Exactly," he said as he slipped on his jacket. "Why are they so uptight? Look at me...I'm relaxed. Let's fucking do this."

I texted Katie to meet us in the lobby as we headed toward the elevator. It's pretty difficult to get arrested on Bourbon Street. You basically have to piss on a cop or murder an étouffée vendor in plain sight. It's nearly impossible to get arrested *anywhere* when you look good in a blazer and have superhuman argumentative powers obtained with quality stimulants. We were ready to show the city who's boss.

When Katie came downstairs the look of frightened bewilderment had faded, which meant she had either bonded with the female roomie or was blackout drunk (possibly both). Regardless, she was comfortable, which was great news for me.

"All right, are you girls ready to see what New Orleans has to offer?" I asked.

"Yes! Let's get some food, we're totally starving!" said Katie.

"Well fuck, you two look good enough to eat! Am I right, Townes?" yelled Nate, awkwardly trying to mask his mental state.

His date giggled bashfully, and I shook my head in disbelief. Katie took my arm and we strolled out onto Bourbon to get dinner, where the real shit-show would begin.

We had a party of twelve, and dinner got belligerent quickly. New Orleans isn't known as a quiet city, but we were by far the most loudmouthed patrons in the establishment. I maintained inebriation with bourbon on the rocks, and the girls all ordered their shitty girly whatever-the-fucks. Not a single one of us was carded. The waiter knew, based on our attire and drunken demeanor, that we were about to spend big money. Katie spilled her drink all over the girl next to her immediately upon receiving it. I laughed hysterically and hit Nate with a fist bump as we watched Katie rub the victim's legs down with napkins. Sluts. Thanks to the heated adrenaline pumping through my body due to the mix of amphetamines and alcohol, I repeatedly left the table to rip cigs. The wait staff was having trouble keeping up with the frequency of our drink orders, and Turbo, whose eyes were occupied by the murderous rage that fills him when he holds an empty beverage, started shouting at busboys and random passersby.

"PABLO! HURRICANES! NOW!"

Everyone gorged on delicious Cajun food, washing down the spiciness with drink after drink. I forced down bites, relieved of hunger by the uppers I had consumed. Things were starting to get hazy, and we had definitely overstayed our welcome, so we asked for the check: $2,275.

It was time for credit card roulette. Turbo dumped the contents of his date's purse out onto the table, and as she yelled at him we each threw our plastic into it. The first card was drawn, and it was mine, saving more money for strippers and gambling. I slammed my drink onto the table in a fit of celebration, and it shattered in an explosion of bourbon and ice. As I turned to look for a waiter, my conscience raised a little red "maybe you should slow down" flag in my mind. I grabbed a random drink off a passing server's tray, told my conscience to go fuck itself, and watched as the game went on.

Only Nate and Turbo remained, staring each other down like whiskey-bent outlaws in a western face-off. Turbo's card was drawn, and he grabbed it with a victorious "FUCK YES" while he held his middle finger in the unlucky loser's face. Naked Nate hung his head in defeat and footed the bill as he muttered, "Fuck it, I'll win it back at the casino."

Night had fallen, and we stumbled out of the restaurant.

The street was littered with extremely questionable and shady characters, as per usual, and our group of well-dressed rageaholics stood out like a wealthy sore thumb, further boosting our elitist aura. Immediately, we devised a plan to send our underage dates to a bar with some of the younger guys so we could hit Harrah's casino and focus on gambling without distractions. I gave Katie a don't-blow-anyone-else reminder makeout, and told her we'd meet up in an hour.

"Don't stay too long. I'll get lonely without you," she flirted as she winked at me.

"I'm just going for a little while so I can win you some spending money for shopping tomorrow, then I'll be back," I assured her. "I promise."

We rushed into the casino like a pack of fiends in need of a fix, and when the sound of shuffling chips and spinning wheels hit our ears, we all imagined the same thing: making it rain thousands in winnings. Within fifteen minutes at our first craps table, I was down 500 bucks, Nate had given up another $1.5K (still fratting in the face of adversity), and Turbo was forced to leave the table after his dripping nosebleed got on the felt. When they kindly asked him to step away, he screamed obscenities at the pit boss, citing a brain tumor as cause for his condition, threatening to sue.

"This is a goddamn travesty! I'm a sick man!" A partially true statement.

I considered myself up a couple grand after escaping credit card roulette, so I started tripling my bets. Strangers were retreating from the tables we had taken over as we blew money pounding scotch and cigars. Two honeymooners from Kansas looked particularly distraught with our behavior. With a roll of the dice and two lungs filled with smoke, Nate addressed them.

"Don't beat that up too hard tonight. She's second-wife material."

They eyed us in astonishment and scurried away. It was time we got the fuck out of there before we were blacklisted. Naked Nate refused to leave the table, and I knew it was likely he'd remain all night, desperately trying to recoup. The rest of us hit the restroom, keyed a couple bumps of instant energy, and bailed back onto Bourbon.

Our next stop was Love Acts, possibly the most disgusting strip club south of the Mason-Dixon. As we made our approach, one of our younger members was getting tossed out. Apparently he'd gotten a little handsy with a stripper and tried to slip her a rogue finger during a backroom lap dance. We posted up around the center stage, swallowing scotch like water, and a full-blown money-spending race had begun. As I rained twenties down on a stripper named "Diamond Cream," my conscience returned and smacked me in the face with a momentary flash of responsibility. I couldn't help but wonder what Katie was doing. I looked over at Turbo, and he had his face sandwiched between a stripper's oversized ass cheeks.

"Jesus, this is nauseating," I accidentally said aloud.

"What's that, baby?" Diamond Cream inquired.

"Fuck." I was surprised she'd heard me. "I said you need Jesus."

I pulled Turbo's head from the jiggling ass sandwich and told him it was time we found our girls. He grabbed the other guys and we headed for the exit, much to the dismay of the pole pros working the stage.

Once we were outside I checked my iPhone and found an excessive eighteen missed calls and repetitive texts from Katie filled with horrific spelling inaccuracies, caused by drunken dyslexia.

1:00 a.m.: *Whats up*

1:10 a.m.: *Townessss where r u*

1:36 a.m.: *Uhhhhh Whatever*

1:45 a.m.: *woohooo! shots shots shots shots shots!*

2:18 a.m.: *Meet us Pat O's!*

2:26 a.m.: *OMG I lobe this gucking bar! Come heee!*

2:45 a.m.: *sick of old men hittig on me I want you bad*

I could barely see straight, but in deciphering her messages I was fairly certain she wanted me to punch my ticket to pound town. I led the group as we plowed through the boisterous crowd toward Pat O'Brien's. Once inside, we figured it'd be pretty difficult to find the girls, but we were wrong. I immediately spotted them onstage with the band, jumping around like crazed groupies at a Beatles concert, with fifteen creepy old men staring up at them from below. As I was making my way toward her, Katie picked me out of the crowd and immediately jumped down, screaming.

"TOWNESSSS! Oh. My. God. Where have you been? This place is so great!"

"Well, one of the guys got sick at the casino, so we had to make sure he was okay," I lied.

"Aw, what a Debbie Downer."

She kissed me, and tasted like a shot of vodka. She was clearly wasted, so I was relieved when she suggested we head back to the hotel to initiate the after-party. I grabbed her hand and led her back through the crowd toward our temporary home.

We assembled at the hotel bar, but had no clue as to the whereabouts of Nate or his date. I ordered a couple shots, decided there was no way I was giving Katie anything else to drink, and ended up taking both of them. Then I tried to dance with her, which consisted of me holding her up while she swayed back and forth like a hippie who's had one too many hits of bad acid.

"Let's just fucking go upstairs," she demanded with drunken feistiness. "I want to play."

Jackpot. She was basically deadweight as we staggered to the hotel room. Good thing I found her, because she would've been an easy target for anyone eyeing her onstage. In the elevator on the way up to our room she hit her head on the wall, then slid to the ground like she'd been shot. The definition of class personified. I pulled her up and held her until we reached our floor, then we made our way toward the room.

After spending ten minutes finding the fucking keycard that was oddly hidden in my pack of cigs, I swiped the thing and attempted to open our door. It was latched shut, so I kicked it in. Welcome to the danger zone. Porn was blaring on the TV, Nate's date was passed out in the shower fully clothed, and Naked Nate himself was passed out on the floor in the middle of the room, completely naked with his flaccid pecker in hand. Katie face-planted onto our bed without concern for the situation. I turned off *Butt Pirates of the Caribbean*, which was ordered for $29.99, and tried to wake Captain Dumbass.

"Hey! WAKE THE FUCK UP!"

I kicked him a few times, but he didn't budge.

"Dude, WAKE UP! COME ON!"

When I leaned over to see if he was breathing, I noticed a puddle of white, creamy liquid crusting over on his stomach.

"Oh fuck! Nate, what the shit did you do?"

He responded with a deep, drawn-out groan, unable to conjure up the English language. At this point I was furious, so I threw a towel over the disgusting bum and started hitting him with a pillow as hard as I could. He finally stirred, then rose like a zombie, took one glassy-eyed look at me, and climbed into bed next to Katie—immediately passing out.

"Oh, okay. Fuck you guys. I'm out of here," I stood and said to my three unconscious friends.

The scenario was far too depressing for me to end my night with, so I bailed.

Back in the hallway, I immediately got a huge whiff of a very distinct and familiar smell. Someone was turning their room into a greenhouse. I roamed aimlessly, following the scent, and banged on the door closest to the odor. Luckily, it was one of our sophomore members, Craig (pre-med), who invited me in, coughing smoke in my face and grinning like a senile mad scientist.

"Townes! Come on in! Join the party."

I entered, praying the situation wasn't similar to the room I had just exited. Apparently Craig had made friends with a couple local performers after a show, because "the party" was comprised of two aspiring rappers, two strippers, and there was no sign of a second roommate or anyone's dates.

The sunlight had begun to peek through the blinds, and I was in the midst of an epic comedown. I definitely needed some of the medicine this unusual ensemble possessed.

"Hit this shit, dude, it'll make you feel better," Craig said.

You don't have to tell me twice, Doctor. I went face deep into a gravity bong, took a hit, and the second I leaned back I knew I was fucked. Until that moment I had managed to successfully balance the mixture of sleep deprivation, uppers, downers, and hand grenades that had flooded my system, but my body had reached its limit.

"Oh shit! White boy can't handle his weed!" yelled one of the strippers.

"Dude, are you okay? Be cool." Thanks for the advice, Craig.

I was so fucking stoned I couldn't even open my mouth to speak, so I nodded like a mute kid with a learning disability. Blacking in and out, I rammed through the door into the hallway and fell over into an ice machine. I tried to stand back up but collapsed, easing my way toward my room with the wall as a crutch. I swiped my card over and over trying to get inside, and realized it was the wrong fucking room.

My conscience chimed back in: *Who's telling who to go fuck himself now? Amateur clown.*

I could hear my brain counting down the seconds until shutdown. 10, 9, 8, 7...Fuck, I needed to find my room. I tried the next door, and it swung open. 6, 5, 4...I fell to my knees and started crawling, then my face hit the carpet as I felt the door close on my feet. 3 . . . 2 . . . 1. Shutdown.

I woke to the sound of Katie's voice.

"Townes?"

Her foot nudged me in the ribs.

"Townes!"

"I'm up, I'm up."

I peeled my head up off the carpet and pulled my feet in through the door, letting it close behind me.

"What the hell happened last night?" she whispered with a concerned sternness. "And why are you sleeping in the doorway?"

"I was with Craig and some—never mind. What time is it?"

"Nine-thirty in the morning. I woke up next to Nate, and he was . . . he was . . ."

"Naked?" I asked, smirking. "Yeah, I saw that."

I got to my feet and saw that Naked Nate was still out cold in my bed, his date had found her way to what was supposed to be their bed, and Katie was already dressed and ready for the day.

"You want to get breakfast?" she asked. "You look like you need it."

"Thank you and yes, yes I do. Let me change and we'll get out of here."

At the hotel's complimentary breakfast we ate with a bunch of the younger guys and their dates, and I was updated on the rest of the events from the previous evening. These were the stats:

Three groups were evicted from their rooms for receiving multiple noise complaints. They moved to the Holiday Inn two blocks away.

Five guys got into a fight outside Razzoo's bar at 4:30 in the morning with some Deltas from Oregon after an argument about football.

One of our freshmen, James Perry, spent $3,600 in the Penthouse Club VIP room after he caught his date making out with a random guy.

A sophomore nicknamed "Bull" broke his arm falling down the stairs of the hotel. Apparently security had found him standing with his eyes closed in the elevator on the fifth floor, not pressing any buttons, and asked him what floor he was trying to reach. He opened his eyes, panicked, ran out of the elevator, pushed open the door to the staircase, and fell down the stairs. He spent all night in the ER.

In the end it was a historically successful trip. New Orleans was a city built for frat moves, and we kept the tradition alive and well to the best of our abilities. We gave it our all, left it all on the playing field, and went home without any regrets. Stories from our trip would be told to rushees for years to come, and pictures would circulate through Facebook and Twitter, threatening to end political careers for some guys before they'd even begun. It was an incomparable final formal to cap off my active membership as an Alpha, and the exclamation point at the end of the best years of my life.

––––––

Fraternity formals are one of the great oxymorons of society. Hundreds of guys and girls dress in their finest suits and dresses, and then get completely obliterated, gradually deformalizing their outfits by the night's end. But they look damn good doing it...

On Fashion and Formals

The better you dress, the worse you can behave. TFM.

This blazer gives me confidence I don't even need. TFM.

The grin you get when your professor asks, "So did anyone do anything fun this weekend?" TFM.

Sneaking drugs past cops by hiding them in my bloodstream. TFM.

The blazer chest-pocket beer. TFM.

Landing a haymaker at the bar in a sports coat. TFM.

Smoking weed in a bowtie. TFM.

Any occasion worth wearing a blazer is worth bringing a flask. TFM.

Carrying uppers in the coin pocket of your khakis. TFM.

Went to a pajama party in khakis and a button-down because that's usually what I pass out in. TFM.

Riding the ice sculpture at formal. TFM.

"A little bit softer now." TFM.

Formal shotguns. TFM.

Getting weird at formal gatherings. TFM.

Not giving a single fuck at formal. TFM.

The morning after. TFM.

Epilogue

THE VERY NEXT WEEK AFTER OUR FORMAL IN NEW ORLEANS I became an official alumnus of Alpha. I had paid my dues in full and been an active member of the fraternity for the maximum of four years, so that was it. It was all over. I even spent another year on campus, but I was more focused on graduation than blacking out and slaying randoms. The good times had come to an end and the real world was calling.

It was incredibly depressing, because I knew the truth. I knew I'd graduate, get a great job, marry a total smokeshow, have athletic kids, and build a life for myself that 99 percent of the world would envy, but things would never be the same. When my firstborn enters this world I'm sure I'll say it's "the happiest day of my life," but will I really be happier than I was being showered with beer in the middle of a party with three hundred people screaming at the top of their lungs around me while I've got two hands full of tits? Probably not. The real world comes with real responsibilities, taxes, career choices, and mature women who know better.

But when I'm an old man, retired and knocking over picture frames with my medicated boner, I'll still think back to those nights I had with Monte, Turbo, Nate, and all my other friends, and smile when I think about how good we had it. No matter how much time passes, or how things change, nobody can take those years away from us. Nationals might crack down on hazing, universities might ban alcohol on campuses, schools might do away with fraternities altogether, but they can never take away what we had. Did we act irresponsibly? Sure. Did we piss some people off along the way? Definitely. Did most of us almost die? Yes. Would I go back and do it all again? In a fucking heartbeat.

My birth certificate says I'm 19 years old. My ID says I'm 25 years old. My wardrobe says I'm 43 years old. TFM.

Being the peer who pressures. TFM.

Ordering food delivery, then passing out before it arrives. TFM.

Giving condescending nicknames to people you barely know. TFM.

"How old are you?" really means "I want to fuck you, but I don't want to go to jail." TFM.

People call me by my first and last name with "fucking" in the middle. TFM.

Overdressed and under the influence. TFM.

Studying is for people who don't trust their instincts. TFM.

"2 hour parking" sign over my bed so they know they're not welcome to stay the night. TFM.

Told the GDI in front of me, "Hey do you want to split the work? I'll do 1-5 and you do 6-10." Told the GDI behind me, "Hey do you want to split the work? I'll do 6-10 and you do 1-5." TFM.

"Here, put your number in. I don't know how to spell your name." TFM.

We gave up on coming up with a witty name for the party, so the theme was "Ex-Athletes and Sluts." TFM.

The band from last year refused to return because of my behavior towards them. If they had played "Free Bird" there wouldn't have been a problem. TFM.

I like my women like my whiskey, 18 years old and mixed up with coke. Just kidding, I would never do that to the whiskey. TFM.

"I'll quit after college." TFM.

I don't pay for my friends. I pay for a mansion where we throw parties that you're not invited to. TFM.

Never helping with group projects, but always being the one who presents them. TFM.

Public display of erection. TFM.

Better late than sober. TFM.

Awoke this morning with my slampiece in one arm and a half empty bottle of Maker's Mark in the other. Guess which one joined me for breakfast. TFM.

Waiting for rush to be over so I can take a 4-month break from having to bend over and tie my own shoes. TFM.

The perfect blend of complete gentleman and total asshole. TFM.

Slamming like it's the 60s, getting high like the 70s, dressing like the 80s, making money like the 90s, and drinking like it's the end of the world. TFM.

"I really shouldn't do this." Spoiler alert: she does it. TFM.

Telling the rushee with pierced ears that the house is closed when there is obviously a full-blown rager going on. TFM.

My relationships are like trick candles. She can blow me all she wants but we'll never go out. TFM.

Telling GDIs to come back when we have an open party. We never have an open party. TFM.

Sorostitutes aren't allowed over during "sorority silence." Luckily, strippers are always welcome. TFM.

If I wanted to be your friend I would've given you a bid. TFM.

Using your one phone call to order pizza for everyone in the drunk tank. TFM.

Impressing the mother on the dance floor, and then impressing the daughter in the bedroom. TFM.

Waking up from a blackout with a ruler duct taped to what feels like a broken ankle. TFM.

I trust my pledge brothers with my life, but I keep a padlock on my liquor cabinet. TFM.

Diagnosing every injury sustained by a brother as "a broken vagina." TFM.

Telling someone "I'll see what I can do" when the situation is clearly out of control. TFM.

"It was like that when we got here." TFM.

Goths call us conformists. Hipsters call us mainstream. PETA calls us cruel. Environmentalists call us close-minded. Feminists call us womanizers. Socialists call us greedy. Liberals call us ignorant. But despite all this, society calls us successful. TFM.

Suits and boots. TFM.

Swinging for the fences. TFM.

The one-handed keg stand. TFM.

Alumni relations. TFM.

The frat pile. TFM.

Using cargo shorts to light your cigarette. TFM.

Beer bonging at sunrise. TFM.

Fighter pilot beer bongs. TFM.

Frat boarding. TFM.

Having the captain stow a keg. TFM.

Studying abroad. TFM.

Being "that guy." TFM.

Acknowledgments

First and foremost, I'd like to thank Madison Wickham and Ryan Young for founding TotalFratMove.com, hiring me so that I didn't have to get a real job, and trusting me with the opportunity to write this book.

I'd like to thank our agent, Byrd Leavell, without whom none of this would've been possible. Byrd reached out to us at TFM knowing there was an opportunity for this book to exist, and then gave me a shot at writing it. His foresight and step-by-step guidance was essential, and I am eternally grateful.

I'd also like to thank our editor, Ben Greenberg, his assistant, Pippa White, and everyone at Grand Central for their unparalleled professionalism and dedication to this project. Also, Roland Ottewell for his expert copyediting, and Catherine Casalino for her work on the cover.

Additional thanks to Rob, Dillon, Andrew, Eric, Barrett, Taylor, Thomas, Megan, Ilene, Everett, JaNae, Courtney, Ashley, Chelsea, my little brother Sam, and everyone else who helped out in some way, shape, or form.

I'd also like to give an enormous thank-you to my parents, and my entire family, for not disowning me between the years 2005–2010.

And one last huge thank-you to the guys I can't name who actually lived the inspiration for this book with me.